"In *Blessed Are the Unsatisfied*, Amy Simpson considers questions many Christians think about but have been unwilling or unable to openly express. In her personal and engaging style, Amy encourages us to embrace the unsatisfied life because it leads to greater intimacy with the only one who is able to satisfy. A must-read for any believer struggling to live out the 'Christian life.'"
Matthew S. Stanford, author of *Grace for the Afflicted*

"In *Blessed Are the Unsatisfied*, Amy Simpson puts a positive spin on what is usually perceived as a negative state of mind. She avoids making unrealistic promises of full and perfect satisfaction in this fallen world, as some are inclined to do. Instead, she shows how 'unsatisfaction' can motivate us to pursue a deeper relationship with God and with others, to learn, grow, and change ourselves, and to invest our energies in making this world a better place for others. Seems we could all use a little more unsatisfaction."
Carolyn Custis James, author of *Half the Church* and *Malestrom*

"The first emotion I had reading *Blessed Are the Unsatisfied* was sheer relief. Raised in the church, I've heard a thousand glib assurances that anyone who trusts Jesus for salvation will be completely satisfied—and I've despaired a thousand times as I've felt that satisfaction elude me. How freeing to hear that being unsatisfied doesn't mean I'm a defective Christian! The second emotion I felt was hope. Simpson gave me permission to stay hungry for ultimate satisfaction while providing strategies for pursuing the abundant life of which Jesus spoke."
Drew Dyck, senior editor, CTPastors.com, author of *Yawning at Tigers*

"The truth is that there are promises of Jesus that are 'here and now, but not yet thoroughly experienced' until we are in heaven. Amy Simpson does an exceptional job of digging deep into God's Word and exposes the truth that we are not completely satisfied in Jesus in this life."
Brad Hoefs, president, Fresh Hope for Mental Health

Blessed Are the
Unsatisfied

Finding Spiritual Freedom
in an Imperfect World

AMY SIMPSON

IVP Books

An imprint of InterVarsity Press
Downers Grove, Illinois

InterVarsity Press
P.O. Box 1400, Downers Grove, IL 60515-1426
ivpress.com
email@ivpress.com

InterVarsity Press® is the book-publishing division of InterVarsity Christian Fellowship/USA®, a movement of students and faculty active on campus at hundreds of universities, colleges, and schools of nursing in the United States of America, and a member movement of the International Fellowship of Evangelical Students. For information about local and regional activities, visit intervarsity.org.

All Scripture quotations, unless otherwise indicated, are taken from The Holy Bible, New International Version®, NIV®. Copyright © 1973, 1978, 1984, 2011 by Biblica, Inc.™ Used by permission of Zondervan. All rights reserved worldwide. www.zondervan.com. The "NIV" and "New International Version" are trademarks registered in the United States Patent and Trademark Office by Biblica, Inc.™

While any stories in this book are true, some names and identifying information may have been changed to protect the privacy of individuals.

Cover design: David Fassett
Interior design: Jeanna Wiggins
Images: blue watercolor: © saemilee/iStockphoto
> *drinking glass: © limpido/iStockphoto*
> *paper background: © GOLDsquirrel/iStockphoto*

ISBN 978-0-8308-4497-5 (print)
ISBN 978-0-8308-9238-9 (digital)

Printed in the United States of America ∞

InterVarsity Press is committed to ecological stewardship and to the conservation of natural resources in all our operations. This book was printed using sustainably sourced paper.

Library of Congress Cataloging-in-Publication Data
A catalog record for this book is available from the Library of Congress.

P	21	20	19	18	17	16	15	14	13	12	11	10	9	8	7	6	5	4	3	2	1
Y	35	34	33	32	31	30	29	28	27	26	25	24	23	22	21	20	19	18			

THIS BOOK IS DEDICATED TO . . .

Trevor, who is my very favorite person, who has taught me so much about Jesus through the way he lives, and who still is the one I would choose to be my partner in this unsatisfied life.

My two daughters, for whom I dream many things, the greatest of which is a hunger and thirst that will keep them in pursuit of a life in relationship with the true Source of satisfaction beyond this life.

With all thanks and gratitude to God, who gives my life its only real meaning and continually calls me toward a deeper and less satisfied version of myself.

Contents

INTRODUCTION

I Still Haven't Found What I'm Looking For

꽃

I'm a Christian, and I am unsatisfied with my life. I hope you're unsatisfied too.

You see, I don't subscribe to the common belief that once our souls get right with God, we will be deeply, completely satisfied in this life we're living. In fact, I think the opposite is true: the more we know God and find ourselves longing for what he wants for us, the less we feel truly at home in the places and times we inhabit.

This may sound like bad news, but embracing an unsatisfied life throws the gospel into relief, highlighting how much we need God to rescue us. And living an unsatisfied life has its upsides—including freedom from the pursuit of something we will not achieve in this life. So if you're like me and you have found true satisfaction elusive, or if you have been afraid to acknowledge that you still live with a deep sense of longing, you're in good company right now.

Back in my preteen and teenage years, I found I just couldn't buy into some of the prevailing stories I heard repeated in my broader Christian community. These messages were too simple, too neat in their claims—including the claim that Christians should be happier than everyone else, fearless, and consistently radiant in our peaceful stroll toward heaven, all our longings fulfilled. They didn't match what I saw of the world, didn't match what I read in my Bible. They didn't match what I saw in my own family.

You see, my family had always been different, and my mother in particular had always been different from other moms. But I didn't know she had a serious mental illness until I was fourteen years old, when she finally had a psychotic episode so severe it left her debilitated. It left my family permanently changed, and I couldn't deny that our experience absolutely didn't fit the prevailing picture of the faithful Christian life, which goes something like this: You repent and accept God's grace. You immediately enjoy a sense of peace and happiness that is always with you. You read the Bible, go to church, and pray as much as possible, and over time Christ will painlessly transform you into a person more like him. You grow in knowledge, faith, and joy. You're not supposed to be derailed by debilitating emotions, faulty thinking, or paranoid delusions. You don't suffer deeply, in ways that completely alter the rest of your life, in ways that you just can't manage gracefully. If you do suffer, you're supposed do so quietly, to quickly find meaning in it, experience God's healing, and move on. You're supposed to be deeply and joyfully satisfied, completely fulfilled by a relationship with God, which means you no longer need anything in this life beyond a connection with his presence. Life becomes an ongoing celebration, unclouded by lament or loss.

The persistent anguish of repeatedly losing someone I loved affirmed to me that I did need something more than just a relationship with God in this life. While it's true God is a mother to the motherless, nothing replaced that missing relationship. And while being essentially motherless is not a fatal condition, it has a lasting impact; it leaves scars that are always sensitive. So if I was going to believe any story about God being with his people and meeting all their needs, it was going to have to accommodate a story like mine.

Some days during my teenage years, life was excruciating. I was deeply unsatisfied with life as it was unfolding. I was serious about growing in my relationship with Christ, yet I found I still had unmet longings; I remained hungry and thirsty for spiritual fulfillment and for a life better than the one I lived.

My family was living on public assistance, food pantry fare, government cheese, and the discounted bread that had passed its expiration date. I believed that if only I had what other people had, my spiritual and emotional hunger would be quelled. My mother was ill and dependent on me and my siblings, and I thought that if only I had a normal family I would no longer thirst for a more fulfilling life. I lived in the country, then in the city, in decidedly ordinary and overlooked places. I dreamed that if I could go to the exciting and glamorous places, or become one of the suburban folks I envied, I would feel like I belonged in this world.

I got some of what I wanted. I went to college, got married, became a professional, earned an adequate income, experienced some success. I became a mother myself, had some adventures, even moved to the suburbs. I went to counseling, did some hard work to heal from the hardships of my youth, even wrote a book sharing my family's story, which God turned into a ministry to many people like us. I studied the Bible, spent a lot of time in prayer, and served in the church. And I am here to tell you that I am still not satisfied—not by my life's circumstances and not by my relationship with God.

Along the way, I learned that life can be deeply fulfilling, but the church was right when it taught me that what this world offers does not satisfy. And my early suspicions about some of the church's promises were right too. In some ways my spirit is hungrier and thirstier today than it was when I was a child repenting of sin for the first time and believing Jesus would make me happy. I now know that my appetite for God's presence has grown as I have indulged it and grown to know him more. The more I know Jesus and learn from him, the more I long to know him and be united with him. The closer my relationship with him, the less satisfied I am with that relationship.

Statistics suggest I have a lot of life ahead of me. I plan to be far more intimate with Jesus at the end of my life than I am today, thanks to the work I know the Holy Spirit will do in me in the intervening years. Yet when I imagine myself on my deathbed, comforted by a sense of Immanuel, I picture myself as both very close to Jesus and longing for him more deeply than ever. Don't get me wrong; I am moving into greater unity and connection with Christ, thanks to his gracious persistence. But even as Jesus moves me closer to satisfaction in him, I still live with a kind of unsatisfaction that will not be lifted in this life.

Your story is different. You have been down a road I wouldn't even recognize. But I am certain you have met with disappointment and loss, and you know what it is to long for a life without moments of emptiness, weariness, insecurity, discord, and the occasional feeling that God is far away. Like me, you may have heard many times that real Christians don't have such longings.

Christian teachers and leaders point out the shortcomings of what this world can offer us and point people toward Jesus with a faulty promise. "Only Jesus will satisfy," they say. The satisfied life is found in living God's way, and when we come to him for fulfillment we will find it. But Jesus doesn't fulfill all our longings in this life. Instead, he offers us his peace. Jesus does not remove us from the fog of death and the ongoing consequences of human rebellion against God. He does not give us a "get out of suffering free" card.

He gives us purpose and reconciles us to the God we were created to know and love. He redeems our suffering and uses it to re-form us. He reshapes our desires and changes us from the inside out. But he does not make us comfortable with life amid decay, death, depravity, and disappointment. Why would he want to do that?

When we wake up in the morning with the expectation of satisfaction, we're trying to make this world into a place it can't be. When we believe Jesus should satisfy us, we come before him with our paltry demands and miss what he actually wants to give us. When we tell the world that simply knowing Jesus or following God's ways of living brings satisfaction and fulfills all our needs, we mislead them; we encourage them to come to Jesus as consumers, and we set them up to walk away when he doesn't deliver on the sales pitch.

Most of us have moments of satisfaction. We experience happiness, joy, and life-giving connections with God and other people. We find meaning in life. We enjoy times of fulfillment. We can take pleasure in God's good gifts and be content with our circumstances. And when we surrender to our Creator, we find a purpose and pattern to our lives that makes them far richer than they were previously. But all these experiences are transitory, and they do not add up to a deep, overriding, constant, soul-deep satisfaction that removes all our longings and conquers our human limitations. That's the kind of satisfaction I'm talking about. And something is wrong if we believe we can live with that kind of satisfaction—or that we should achieve it in this life.

So what are we to do? Give up? Simply bide our time—or waste it—until we can live in God's presence and experience satisfaction?

On the contrary, we can endure the curse and learn to embrace the blessings of the unsatisfied life. We are promised good things when we live unsatisfied, hungry and thirsty for righteousness, and I invite you on a journey to explore those blessings. I invite you to consider intentionally living unsatisfied.

Jesus Doesn't Want You to Be Satisfied . . . Yet

1

❦

TV preachers such as Kenneth Copeland tell us what many of us most want to hear: "God intends for you to be satisfied in every area of your life."

For Joel Osteen, pastor of the largest church in the United States, finding spiritual, emotional, and even material satisfaction in a relationship with God is at the core of what it means to be a Christian. "God wants you to live a satisfied life," he writes.

> He wants you to have a life filled with an abundance of joy, an abundance of happiness. God doesn't want you simply to survive that marriage. God wants to turn it around and restore you with a strong, healthy, rewarding relationship. God doesn't want your business to merely make it through the murky economic waters. He wants your

business to sail and to excel! When God restores, He always brings you out better, improved, increased, and multiplied. He has a vision of total victory for your life!

Christian teacher Joyce Meyer presents a similar formula for Christian living: "God cares about everything about you and everything that concerns you. He wants to be good to you and He will never disappoint you. Give Him all of your heart and put all of your hope and expectation in Him. You can have true contentment and satisfaction in Christ!" She promises big emotional benefits from obedience: "I encourage you to let God shape you into someone who loves and actually longs for His correction. Because by bending to His will, we can become healed and whole, satisfied and happy."

Many people interpret these promises to mean getting what they want. But getting what we want doesn't deliver what we think it will. Open a search engine and type "It didn't make me happy," and you'll find stories of people getting married, getting divorced, having a family, finding and losing jobs, converting to one religion or another, gaining and losing weight, making money, giving it away, moving from one place to another, reaching career goals. You'll find story after story of people getting what they want and finding it didn't give them what they thought it would. If you keep looking, you might find the story of Donna Mikkin, who achieved what many people are dreaming of: she won the lottery.

In 2007, Donna and her husband, Ed, won $34.5 million through the New York State Lottery. And now she says, "My life was hijacked by the lottery." Far from improving her life, the windfall made things worse. "Most of us think that winning the lottery is the ultimate fulfillment. But I found that wasn't the case. Most people look at winning the lottery as some magic pot of gold waiting for you at the end of the rainbow." But it brought her no peace, happiness, or contentment, and she became a person she didn't want to be.

Lest you believe Donna is an isolated case, consider this. Experts say 70 percent of people who win the lottery (or otherwise come to a sudden windfall of money) are bankrupt within five years. Some lottery winners learn to manage their wealth and don't regret their wins, but many, like Donna, feel like anything but winners. Their lives are dogged by mistrust, anxiety, and the consequences of foolish choices. Some meet with violence, others with constant requests for money. Some say their winnings are cursed. Others simply don't like the person they see in the mirror. They say things like "I don't like what I've become" and "I'd have been better off broke."

Multiple studies have shown that while people may feel happier once they rise above the poverty level, beyond that, more money does not generally improve people's sense of well-being. Psychologists point to various reasons why having more money doesn't necessarily make people happier than they were before—and can actually make people miserable. One is the idea of experience stretching, the concept that as we are able to enjoy more of what money can buy, we enjoy the simpler pleasures in life less. So the things people used to enjoy before winning the lottery no longer give them joy.

In one classic study, conducted in the 1970s, researchers compared lottery winners with people who had recently suffered severe injuries that had left them with either partial or total paralysis. The study found that these accident victims derived more pleasure from everyday activities than the lottery winners. As the study's authors explained, "Eventually, the thrill of winning the lottery will itself wear off. If all things are judged by the extent to which they depart from a baseline of past experience, gradually even the most positive events will cease to have impact as they themselves are absorbed into the new baseline against which further events are judged." In other words, we have a tendency to adjust our expectations, and our standard of what will make us happy, to match our experiences. Happiness is a moving target.

The stories of miserable lottery winners are about people who bought tickets because they thought winning would make their lives better. And like so many of us, they have discovered a decidedly biblical truth: the places we seek satisfaction often fail to provide it. In fact, they can leave us more miserable.

All we need to do is seek satisfaction in a relationship with Jesus, right?

If you're a Christian and you've been following Jesus for more than three minutes, you may be shocked by the title of this chapter. After all, if orthodox theology is defined by the bestselling Christian books and other media, the idea that Jesus doesn't want us to be satisfied is heresy.

While most Christians freely embrace the idea that the world doesn't satisfy (although most of us—including me—still face temptation to seek satisfaction in various ways in this world), many do believe the remedy is to seek satisfaction in a relationship with Jesus. And they believe that remedy will make their longings disappear. As long as we are in relationship with Jesus, he will fill that "God-shaped hole" inside us, and once that hole is filled, we will no longer ache with desire or longing or a nagging sense of dissatisfaction or spiritual suffering. We have no shortage of Christian pastors, teachers, and other leaders telling us this very thing. While the world doesn't satisfy, they say, Jesus does.

The trouble is, while knowing and following Jesus has its priceless rewards and leads to complete satisfaction, it won't deliver on this promise now. Sometimes obedience makes a person miserable. Sometimes it leads to suffering or even death. Yes, a relationship with God can bring comfort, peace, and even joy in such circumstances. But it may not bring satisfaction or happiness—at least in complete and lasting form.

It's time to question this message.

A GOD-SHAPED HOLE

Way back in the 1600s, French polymath Blaise Pascal wrote on the topic of the human search for happiness. "All men seek happiness," he said. "This is without exception. . . . And yet, after such a great number of years, no one without faith has reached the point to which all continually look." In other words, people have been looking for happiness since the beginning of time, and no one can find it without faith.

"But example teaches us little," he wrote. "While the present never satisfies us, experience dupes us and, from misfortune to misfortune, leads us to death, their eternal crown." Sounds kind of like the book of Ecclesiastes, where we find expressions of disenchantment that are often echoed in the words of disappointed people today:

> I denied myself nothing my eyes desired;
>> I refused my heart no pleasure.
> My heart took delight in all my labor,
>> and this was the reward for all my toil.
> Yet when I surveyed all that my hands had done
>> and what I had toiled to achieve,
> everything was meaningless, a chasing after the wind;
>> nothing was gained under the sun. (Ecclesiastes 2:10-11)

Yet like the writer of Ecclesiastes, Pascal was not hopeless. In fact, he saw this universal quest for happiness and satisfaction as evidence for the truth of Christianity's claims. In his most-often-misquoted passage he wrote:

What is it, then, that this desire and this inability proclaim to us, but that there was once in man a true happiness of which there now remain to him only the mark and empty trace, which he in vain tries to fill from all his surroundings, seeking from things absent the help he does not obtain in things present? But these are all inadequate, because the infinite abyss can only be filled by an infinite and immutable object, that is to say, only by God Himself. He only is our true good, and since we have forsaken him, it is a strange thing that there is nothing in nature which has not been serviceable in taking His place; the stars, the heavens, earth, the elements, plants, cabbages, leeks, animals, insects, calves, serpents, fever, pestilence, war, famine, vices, adultery, incest.

At some point during the three hundred–plus years since Pascal wrote these words, someone decided to paraphrase them for popular consumption: "There is a God-shaped vacuum in the heart of every man which cannot be filled by any created thing, but only by God, the Creator, made known through Jesus." Eventually that paraphrase started passing itself off as the original, and it is now regularly attributed to Pascal. And even less thoughtful is the popular claim that we have "a God-shaped hole" waiting to be plugged.

The more modern paraphrases bring images to mind: people walking around with holes in the middle. When those holes are neatly filled with God, the need is met, the longing is satisfied. Presto! Yet Pascal's point was subtly different. The abyss in us is infinite in its nature, he said. It cannot be filled with what is finite. No matter how many finite materials we throw into it, it will gape within us. Only God, infinite and truly good, possesses the nature and the capability to fill it.

Pascal was right. If we want to have this abyss filled, we must seek good at its source: in God himself. God is our only solution. But that doesn't mean God is simply our missing puzzle piece.

Pascal didn't say that once we come into relationship with God, having been justified—made righteous in God's eyes through faith in Jesus' atoning sacrifice on our behalf—our abyss immediately goes away. He didn't speak of a vacuum being filled with a piece of the exact shape and size necessary to do the job.

Neither did Augustine of Hippo, who wrote centuries before Pascal and whose writings Pascal drew on in his own work. Yet Augustine's words are often used to make a similar "God-shaped hole" point. At the beginning of his *Confessions*, Augustine wrote this often-quoted proclamation: "Thou hast formed us for Thyself, and our hearts are restless till they find rest in Thee."

When this quotation is printed on bookmarks and paperweights and sold in Christian bookstores, it seems to support the God-shaped hole theory. Once our restless hearts find a relationship with God, our restlessness disappears and we rest in fellowship with him . . . right?

Well, if Augustine had embraced that view, he probably wouldn't have written this soon after: "Oh! how shall I find rest in Thee? Who will send Thee into my heart to inebriate it, so that I may forget my woes, and embrace Thee, my only good?" Nor this:

> And sometimes Thou dost introduce me to a most rare affection, inwardly, to an inexplicable sweetness, which, if it should be perfected in me, I know not to what point that life might not arrive. But by these wretched weights of mine do I relapse into these things, and am sucked in by my old customs, and am held, and sorrow much, yet am much held. To such an extent does the burden of habit press us down. In this way I can be, but will not; in that I will, but cannot,—on both ways miserable.

These do not sound like the writings of a man whose God-shaped vacuum was satisfied. It seems Augustine's heart, like mine, still felt restless from time to time.

PROMISES OF SATISFACTION

Many Christian writers and leaders make this claim a staple of
their message. Come to Jesus, they say, and you won't feel restless
anymore. You won't wish for happiness or long for satisfaction. You
won't hunger or thirst. You will be satisfied.

Conduct an Internet search for "knowing Jesus will satisfy" or "a
relationship with Jesus will satisfy" or "Find satisfaction in God,"
and you can spend all day scrolling through devotions, blog posts,
book excerpts, sermons, and uplifting videos promising that the
formula for satisfaction in life is simple: stop seeking satisfaction
in the world around you, follow Jesus, know God, and enjoy complete spiritual and emotional satisfaction (maybe even financial
satisfaction), or at least enjoy the fact that you are now satisfied—
whether you feel it or not. And if you don't feel satisfied, the
problem is that you forgot you are satisfied and went looking for
satisfaction again. But if we are satisfied, why in the world would
we ever even think about going off to look for more? Maybe we
don't feel truly satisfied because we aren't. Maybe God doesn't want
to take away our longings yet.

Even well-respected classics lead us to expect something I don't
believe God wants to deliver in this life. Oswald Chambers's classic
and widely beloved devotional *My Utmost for His Highest* tells us
at the beginning of the year:

> When once we get intimate with Jesus we are never lonely,
> we never need sympathy, we can pour out all the time without
> being pathetic. The saint who is intimate with Jesus will never
> leave impressions of himself, but only the impression that
> Jesus is having unhindered way, because the last abyss of his
> nature has been satisfied by Jesus. The only impression left by
> such a life is that of the strong calm sanity that Our Lord
> gives to those who are intimate with Him.

This is a strong claim, and it sounds like a great way to live. But I can tell you that, while I have a long way to go (and a deep longing to go there), I am intimate with Jesus, and after walking with him for more than forty years, I still feel lonely at times. I frequently need sympathy. Sometimes I am unsatisfied not only with my ability to reflect Jesus but also with the very quality of my intimacy with him. I strongly suspect that the abyss of my nature has not been entirely satisfied by Jesus.

I believe this lack of satisfaction is not a problem (beyond the human condition we hold in common) but rather an indication of spiritual vitality. However, many would disagree. For example, according to Jeff Manion's book *Satisfied*, the solution to my problem is to focus on contentment with what I have, rather than the quest for material gain. Choosing contentment, he says, will bring satisfaction. "Contentment is the cultivation of a satisfied heart," he writes. "It is the discipline of being fully alive to God and to others whatever our material circumstances. Contentment is not achieved through getting everything we want but by training the heart to experience full joy and a deep peace even when we don't have what we want." Contentment is important, and I will discuss it in chapter eight. But being content with what we have is not the same as being completely satisfied by it. A materially satisfied person, content with circumstances and possessions, is not the same as a person with a satisfied spirit. The experience of full joy is elusive in this life, even for the most contented. Is it possible that those who believe they have found it are settling for a shadow meant to bless us now, give us a glimpse of what is to come, and keep us focused on the source of joy until we are filled to capacity in another world?

Christian leaders are right when they claim only God can truly satisfy our souls. Only God even understands what our souls need. But after turning to God with our needs and devoting ourselves to relationship with him, many still feel unsatisfied. When we grow deeper in faith and closer to Jesus, we're likely to find ourselves less—not more—satisfied with life here and now. Does it mean something is wrong with us, our faith is weaker than the faith of the people around us who claim they are satisfied, or we are still living as slaves to sin? Or might it mean things are as they should be?

And what does the Bible have to say about this?

A SPRING OF LIVING WATER

At first glance, a reading of certain Scripture passages seems to support the "God-shaped hole" idea. These passages are often quoted to back up the concept that knowing Christ brings instant satisfaction and a lack of satisfaction indicates a spiritual problem that needs to be corrected. Let's look at the most prominent of these passages, in the Gospel of John.

John 4 tells the story of Jesus' encounter with a Samaritan woman, often called the woman at the well. Jesus met her when he was traveling through Samaria and sat down to rest while his disciples went into town to buy some food. When this woman came to the well to draw water, Jesus shocked her by asking her to share some water with him.

Why was this shocking? John 4:9 tells gives us a glimpse: "'You are a Jew and I am a Samaritan woman. How can you ask me for a drink?' (For Jews do not associate with Samaritans.)" In speaking with this woman, Jesus crossed two well-entrenched social barriers: the barrier between men and women and the barrier between Jews and Samaritans.

But Jesus didn't stop at simply reaching across social barriers. More important, he made some shocking claims about his identity and his ability to satisfy thirst. "If you knew the gift of God and who it is that asks you for a drink," he said, "you would have asked him and he would have given you living water." And when the woman questioned his claim to fame, he told her, "Everyone who drinks this water will be thirsty again, but whoever drinks the water I give them will never thirst. Indeed, the water I give them will become in them a spring of water welling up to eternal life" (John 4:10, 13-14).

Wow, never thirst? Does this mean anyone who turns to Jesus for satisfaction will never again experience longing, sorrow, desire, or restlessness again? Well, no. Jesus offered the woman a source of true sustenance, with a promise of full satisfaction in the eternal realm.

The woman took Jesus' words at face value and begged for the water he mentioned: "Sir, give me this water so that I won't get thirsty and have to keep coming here to draw water" (John 4:15). But Jesus hadn't offered to take away her physical need for water. Nor had he offered to remove her spiritual thirst by giving her a cup of better-quality water, as we sometimes suppose. He had pointed to a better water *source*. The words Jesus used point to the difference between drawing water from a well and drinking it a cupful at a time versus having access to an ever-flowing spring that means you'll never have to go looking for a water source again.

All this talk of thirst and water reminds me of times when I have been tremendously thirsty (and, to be honest, it makes me feel thirsty right now). Many of these times have come while I've been hiking. Whenever I'm planning a hike, like all wise hikers, my number-one concern is ensuring access to enough clean drinking water—not just once, but continuously. That means carrying enough water with me, even if it's heavy. It also means anticipating how much water I'll need, especially when the weather is hot. Along the trail, it takes wisdom and self-discipline to drink enough without chugging it too quickly and leaving myself dry long before the next opportunity to get more.

Last summer, I was hiking with my family in New Hampshire on a hot, humid day. The terrain was tree-lined and shaded, but we were sweating constantly and drinking conservatively, knowing we had to make our water last until the end of the hike. We were so happy when we unexpectedly found a water source at the halfway point—and it wasn't just any water source, but a faucet, requiring no filtering or treatment before drinking. O glorious modern plumbing! After conserving for hours, it felt like an incredible luxury to drink our fill. And when we topped off our water bottles for the return trip, we felt incredibly rich.

It's easy to take water for granted until we find ourselves with a finite supply. Then we realize we need nearly constant access to it.

When we enter into relationship with Jesus, we do not merely drink a cupful from a well of deeply satisfying water, never to thirst again. Instead we gain access to a spring of living water that is available to address our thirst at any time. The contrast between a cup of well water and a spring is important to our understanding of what Jesus promised in this passage. If drinking one cup of God's life-giving water at the moment we believe would satisfy us forever, we would not need a spring. The spring would be a pointless extravagance.

But we do need a spring, and God has provided that source of living water to all followers of Christ because he knows we are thirsty people. Later in the book of John, Jesus again refers to this spring of living water, and this time John made clear exactly what he meant. As he was teaching in the temple courts during the Festival of Tabernacles, "Jesus stood and said in a loud voice, 'Let anyone who is thirsty come to me and drink. Whoever believes in me, as Scripture has said, rivers of living water will flow from within them.' *By this he meant the Spirit*, whom those who believed in him were later to receive" (John 7:37-39, emphasis mine). The Holy Spirit is our spring, the source of living water in all believers, and he makes so much water available to us, it flows out of us in streams that have the capacity to change the world around us.

Yet for the all the spiritual abundance the Holy Spirit provides, Jesus' offer of living water does not promise immediate and full satisfaction. Eighteenth-century Baptist theologian John Gill wrote about Jesus' promise of living water, "Thirsty persons are invited to take and drink of the water of life freely, and are pronounced blessed; and it is promised, that they shall be filled, or satisfied; yet not so in this life, that they shall never thirst or desire more; for as they need more grace, and it is promised them, they thirst after it, and desire it; and the more they taste and partake of it, the more they desire it." In a sense, having this source of living water within makes us even thirstier for what the Holy Spirit offers.

Nineteenth-century Presbyterian minister Marvin Vincent spoke to the phenomenon of increasing, not decreasing, thirst:

> It must not be understood, however, that the reception of the divine life by a believer does away with all further desire. On the contrary, it generates new desires. The drinking of the living water is put as a single act, in order to indicate the divine principle of life as containing in itself alone the satisfaction of all holy desires as they successively arise; in contrast with human sources, which are soon exhausted, and drive one to other fountains.

Anyone who lives with the Holy Spirit knows it's possible for us to choose whether to follow his leading, choose whether to draw on his resources. And anyone who is honest knows we all do this imperfectly, and our spiritual, emotional, relational, and mental thirst does not go away when the Holy Spirit takes up residence in us. Instead, the Holy Spirit acts as a seal on a promise God has made for our future (Ephesians 1:13-14). Someday our thirst will be fully quenched. Someday we will "never thirst"—and that day is not yet here.

Thanks be to God, his people will not suffer unquenched thirst. We don't need to go to the well again; we carry the water around with us in the form of God's Spirit. We need continual access to a source of water because we do continue to thirst, even if we are not characterized as thirsty. We start—not finish—drinking the living water now.

SO WHAT DOES THE BIBLE LEAD US TO EXPECT?

For all the passages that seem to suggest we should expect full and immediate satisfaction when we come into right relationship with God, the Bible contains plenty of passages that give a different message. But more compelling than individual passages are the lives of individuals. When I look in my Bible, I read about a lot of people who seemed to exhibit a marked lack of satisfaction.

Consider just a few of the Old Testament prophets. On the heels of his great victory over the prophets of Baal on Mount Carmel, Elijah ran for his life, became depressed and suicidal, and complained to God (inaccurately) that he was the only faithful prophet left alive (1 Kings 19). Jeremiah, also known as "the weeping prophet," wrote a book called Lamentations. Enough said, but I'll say more. He was hated, rejected, and persecuted for delivering the messages God called him to deliver, and he found himself bemoaning his prophetic calling and cursing the day he was born (Jeremiah 20). At God's command, Hosea married an adulterous prostitute and became a living object lesson of God's love toward his unfaithful people. No complaint is recorded, but it's easy to imagine his life was less than satisfying. Jonah was called out for a special job and in desperation tried to run away from God. After a time of deep repentance and prayer, he committed himself to God's mission; then, when his preaching actually made his audience repent and turn toward God, Jonah was so discouraged he became suicidal. And oddly, that's how Jonah stands as the book ends.

Each of these men was intimate with God, and look where it got them.

What about Jesus himself? What can we learn from his life? Was he satisfied by his life in this world? Did he demonstrate satisfaction for us? The idea is laughable! "He was despised and rejected by mankind, a man of suffering, and familiar with pain" (Isaiah 53:3). He wept over Jerusalem, matter-of-factly told a potential follower that following him would be no picnic, and lost his temper over corruption in the temple. He knew the motives of people who pretended to be interested in his teachings. He knew how vulnerable his friends were and was frustrated with their lack of understanding. And he knew they would all abandon him at the end. When he faced death by crucifixion, he spent the night in prayer. Was he so filled with peace that his coming sacrifice didn't bother him? No way! He told his disciples, "My soul is overwhelmed with sorrow to the point of death." He didn't want to be alone. "Stay here and keep watch," he requested (Mark 14:34).

As one who came from heaven and gave up the privileges of being God to come to earth and face God the Father's rejection, he must have been deeply unsatisfied in this corrupt place, living a sinless life under the heavy shadow of sin's curse, among people who rejected God as a matter of course and missed all the obvious signs of God's nature.

We cannot experience what Jesus experienced. We don't know what it's like to be divine and living among mortals. We'll never understand what it meant for him to don not only human form but humanity itself, with its limitations, pains, and sorrows. But like Jesus, we should be uncomfortable here. We should be unsatisfied by what we experience in this life. We were made for another world, and God wants his people to long for it.

Blessings of the Unsatisfied Life:
THE BLESSING OF NEED

Blessings often don't look the way we expect them to. Left to our wisdom, humans are not quick to seek blessing in curses. But praise be to God, that's the way things work under God's compassion. We are surprisingly blessed in our hunger and thirst.

Unsatisfaction reminds us we need God. Along with its ugly cousin dissatisfaction, unsatisfaction often draws people to church. (For a discussion about the differences between unsatisfaction and dissatisfaction, see chapter two.) And for Christians who have been part of the church for a long time, acknowledging unsatisfaction can lead us to keep going.

I first made a formal commitment to follow Jesus when I was four years old. And yes, I do remember it. I also remember a general fear that I would go to hell and "asking Jesus into my heart" several more times over the next couple of years, just to make sure it took.

I was a spiritually sensitive child, and unlike a lot of pastor's kids, I loved the church (most of the time). Throughout my childhood I grew in my knowledge of God, my understanding of the Bible, and the extent to which my behavior reflected the fruit of the Holy Spirit. But I never truly felt my desperate need of God until I was thirteen and my dad left his job. My family had moved before, but this time I was terrified.

As I've written and spoken about in many places (including in my book called *Troubled Minds: Mental Illness and the Church's Mission),* I grew up in a family marked by serious mental illness. My mom lives with schizophrenia, among the most severe forms of psychiatric disorder. When I was young, I didn't understand that she had an illness—and no one else did either. But I always knew my mom was not able to protect me from danger. I always knew, as far back as I can remember, that in some ways I was stronger than her. For me this reality created not only anxiety but a strong sense of independence and self-reliance that served me well—until it wasn't enough.

Because Dad was a pastor in rural churches, leaving a job meant moving to a different community. And as my family planned our move that year, it became apparent that we might move to the city. I had lived in cities before, but I couldn't remember them; I had lived in rural towns since I was four, and my knowledge of city life came from reading books and watching TV. I was overwhelmed by the thought of so many people, afraid I would be lost in a sea of humanity. I pictured constant crime and danger. Frankly, I was terrified by the prospect.

That fear drove me to get more serious about my relationship with God. I knew my self-sufficiency was insufficient to get me through the challenges I might face. I prayed and told God, "I don't want to go anywhere without you." And I wrote a dated note in the front of my Bible, assuring myself I had made a full-scale commitment to Jesus that day. Boy, did that come in handy.

Most of my fears about city life were mythical and evaporated pretty quickly. Others were well-founded and motivated me to develop some new skills. But I never could have anticipated what unfolded in our new surroundings. Less than one year after I wrote in my Bible, schizophrenia kicked in the door and invaded our lives. In the wake of the stress of our major move and all the trials that went with it, my mom's illness became more profound and obvious, and she began to have severe psychotic episodes, repeated hospitalizations, and disabling treatments. My teenage years were like the worst kind of carnival ride—a series of downward spirals, gut-lurching twists, gnawing fear, and silent screams. My siblings and I felt responsible for each other yet coped like islands. My parents were effectively absent, Dad suffering as much as Mom. I don't know how many times I looked back at that note I wrote in my Bible, seeking assurance that despite the way I sometimes felt, I wasn't walking alone. As with everyone else, it was hardship that kept me in touch with the fact that I needed God.

It's common for people to lose touch with their sense of need when things are going well and they're feeling great. This was human nature in ancient times as much as today, and Moses made reference to it in Deuteronomy 8:11-17. As they stood on the cusp of entering the Promised Land, he told the people of Israel, "Be careful that you do not forget the LORD your God, failing to observe his commands, his laws and his decrees that I am giving you this day. Otherwise, when you eat and are satisfied, when you build fine houses and settle down, and when your herds and flocks grow large and your silver and gold increase and all you have is multiplied, then your heart will become proud and you will forget the LORD your God, who brought you out of Egypt, out of the land of slavery" (Deuteronomy 8:11-14). It's in our times of pain and struggle, when we remember the abyss inside us, that we acutely feel our longing. Even those of us for whom salvation is assured still need to be saved. We can't accomplish this for ourselves, and living unsatisfied can help us remember.

EXERCISES

- Spend some time in worship, making a point to affirm your need for God before asking him for what you want or praying for other people's needs. Consider adding this discipline to your times of worship in the future.

- Make a list of your frequent longings—maybe you often think about a new house or car, a different set of relationships, or an entirely different career. Then take some time to consider the un-fulfilled needs each of these desires might point to. For example, do these longings reflect your need to feel safe, secure, or signif-icant? Many of these needs will never go away in this life; they will be met only through a face-to-face relationship with God in his own unspoiled kingdom. Acknowledge these needs before God and ask him to help you address these needs in healthy ways while accepting unsatisfaction, rather than be driven by an effort to meet those needs in counterproductive ways.

- Write a simple prayer that expresses your need for God. Mem-orize it or place it somewhere where you will see it often. Offer this prayer on a regular basis, especially when things are going well in your life and you might be tempted to forget your deep and unwavering need for God.

Sustainable Faith Is Unsatisfied

Ever since I graduated from college and started my first real job, I have demanded too much of my work. This is completely different from demanding too much work from myself; it's about asking my work to satisfy me in ways it won't. My work is an important part of my life, as I believe it should be. But too often I have made it more than that. I have put my work at the center of my life, seeking meaning and purpose from it. I have asked it to make full use of my gifts and skills while providing constant challenge. And I have expected it to deliver deeply satisfying rewards in proportion to my investment of time, effort, and determination. My career has been a fulfilling one, but thanks to my expectations, I could also look at it as a string of disappointments.

Each time I've changed jobs, I've walked out the door believing I had left most of the unhappiness

in my life behind . . . only to find myself in a new organization just
as imperfect and insufficient as the previous one. And with my
most recent job change came the greatest shock. I moved into full-
time self-employment and was forced to recognize that much of
my work-related angst was still with me. That could only mean one
thing: I was the biggest problem behind the frustrations in my
career. When it came to serving as my own boss, I discovered I was
perfectionistic, demanding, critical, and sometimes indecisive. I
was also humbled.

Being my own boss has been very good for me, partly because I
enjoy what I do. But beyond that, God has used these circumstances to reveal a lot about me—most of which still needs to
change. He has managed to pry my ambitious fingers loose(-ish)
from the controls of my career. And he has helped me grow to a
place of greater balance, in which I turn to my work for satisfaction
and identity less often. The truth is, no matter how successful my
career or how fulfilling my work, it will never satisfy my soul. In
those moments when I place my hopes in my professional accom-
plishments and use them to define my identity and my happiness,
I am always disappointed. I am growing in my understanding that
God has far better purposes for me than simply devoting myself to
building my own kingdom. Why should I settle for less?

Something is wrong if we feel deeply satisfied, or believe we are
satisfied, in this life. Show me those who are completely satisfied
in their intimacy with God, who do not long for much more, and
I'll show you people whose knowledge of God barely scratches the
surface, who have nearly lost sight of heaven, who have forgotten
the first song their soul ever learned to sing, who are much too
easily pleased.

As we look toward a better world, we exercise our faith in what
we cannot see (Hebrews 11:1). And what is visible to us now, we
see as a hazy reflection in a mirror, knowing that someday we will

see face to face and our knowledge—incomplete and unsatisfied for now—will then be complete (1 Corinthians 13:9-12). It's hard to live with faith in what is unseen, yet that is what makes our faith sustainable. It's what produces a faith that can survive, and even thrive, when life is really hard.

Many people, caught up in the pursuit of satisfaction—perhaps even cognitively convincing themselves they are completely satisfied—face a crisis of faith when they run into a brick wall called human life. It's like the reality check that comes with leaving a sheltered environment for the "real world," as my family did when we moved from a rural town to the city. The community we left was part of the real world, but it was a place where kids could be sheltered from some of life's harsh realities. I remember the first day of ninth grade, when my parents took my sisters and me to our new school to register. When we told the principal where we had moved from, she actually sat behind her desk and laughed as if it were the funniest thing she had heard in at least a month. This was not a reassuring introduction. And after leaving the principal's office, it didn't take long to realize I was going to need some new knowledge and skills (like figuring out how to open a locker, understanding that some staircases were reserved for going up and others for going down, and dodging fights in the hallways). I was forced to adapt to an environment very different from the one I had been prepared for.

This kind of shock is inevitable as we go through life. Everyone is affected by the imperfection of human society, the unpredictability (and sometimes tragic predictability) of human behavior, persistent longing, the ridiculous choices we make, the resounding consequences of choices made by someone who came before us. When our understanding of God and ourselves necessitates being satisfied by what we can access now, we will try to make the world's circumstances fit that theology—and we will fail every time. We may grow bitter over perceived injustices from the hand of God (who doesn't seem to be holding up his end of the bargain), become obsessed with controlling other people's behavior to make our illusions achievable, feel overwhelmed by cognitive dissonance, or retreat into a comfortable spiritual coma called denial. The belief that life in this world, in right relationship with God, is as good as we need it to be is incompatible with actual life in this world. It's unsustainable in the face of reality and in the light of what lives in your heart and mine.

HOW SEEKING SATISFACTION HURTS US

When we seek full satisfaction through our faith here and now, we not only settle for less than what God offers us; we also hurt ourselves and our relationship with God. Consider what happens when people expect a relationship with Jesus to bring ultimate satisfaction now.

We expect too much. While our expectations of God can be faulty and unreasonable, we can never overestimate his capabilities. The problem is not a shortcoming in God—far from it! But we can grossly misjudge the possibilities of life on planet earth. When we expect satisfaction here, we attempt to make this world into a place it can't be. We lay on it a weight it can't bear—the weight of utopia, theocracy, or confidence that everything happens for a reason and all works out in the end. Thanks to the consequences of our rebellion against God, we do not live on that planet. Even the most optimistic and sheltered humanist must have moments when his or her philosophies fall apart. For followers of Christ, the limitations of life on earth should come as no surprise.

We complain. When we believe God has promised us satisfaction, it's easy to view discomfort and tragedy as signs that God is not good or not good to us. We may feel justified in complaining about this, and complaining fuels discontentment and more dissatisfaction. We focus on our negative feelings, often blaming God for the consequences of our choices (or someone else's), and we miss the opportunity to live with a God-given sense of purpose.

I recently got together with a friend who was telling me about her workplace, where she is surrounded by complaining coworkers. Her team members don't like their boss, and they have indulged in complaining so often, a spirit of negativity has infected everyone. Complaining has even affected their judgment; no matter what the boss does, it seems like the wrong decision. My friend, who really enjoys her work, finds it hard to go to her job these days because the persistent dissatisfaction wears her out. Anyone who has worked with complainers can relate. It's hard to live and move with excellence and purpose when you're focused on complaints and perceived wrongs.

We behave like spiritual consumers. When we look to the world to satisfy us, we approach life as consumers—people with specific desires, legitimized by the marketplace, shopping around for the products we want. And when we want more, we find it and consume it. The market exists for us and our pleasure. This can also be true of our approach to faith. In some ways our experience of Christ and his church has become a marketplace, with resources and trinkets and churches of all kinds crafting marketing messages to compete for our attention. And for many of us it's easy to move on when we don't like what is said or what they do for us.

When we come to Jesus specifically so he can satisfy us, we keep ourselves in this consumer mindset; we're simply transferring our consumption from the world to Jesus. We come to him with the wrong goal: to find satisfaction rather than to worship and be in right relationship with God because he is God. We too easily believe that he exists for us rather than us for him. But Jesus isn't here for our pleasure. He doesn't come to us on our terms. And he will not be consumed. He insists on transforming us and our desires. If you're a consumer, you probably didn't sign up for that.

We set ourselves up. Sometimes we tell ourselves we're satisfied when we're not, because admitting we aren't feels like admitting we don't know Christ after all. Overestimating our satisfaction can lead us to underestimate our vulnerability to temptation and sin. Our desires have not disappeared, and we all know our good desires are easily corrupted and misdirected. As James tells us, desire is the life source of sin (James 1:15). A lack of awareness of our desires and how those desires might lead us astray can set us up for an easy fall, even if it's gradual.

After all, our sinful, unredeemed natures are still with us. The apostle Paul wrote of our sin natures having been crucified (Galatians 5:24). In a sermon, my pastor, Ray Kollbocker, made an insightful point about the imagery Paul chose: a slow and painful death.

> It seems to me Paul is saying that our sin nature is an incredibly strong and powerful thing and therefore it is not easily or quickly executed. It is an excruciatingly slow and agonizing spiritual process. But when we put our faith in Jesus, that execution—that putting to death of the sin nature—begins. It's not a quick fix; it's not an immediate deal. It is a slow, tortuous struggle because our sin nature with its passions and desires just doesn't want to die.

As followers of Christ, our sin nature is crucified but not yet dead. If our sinful self was truly gone, we would have no need to be wary of our desires. When we fail to recognize how things stand in the meantime, we don't take temptation seriously enough and we encourage hypocrisy as people feel they need to hide their struggles with sin.

We give up. When we expect a relationship with Jesus to satisfy us, we're bound to be disappointed. And for some people this disappointment becomes disenchantment with the church, with

Christianity, with God. We become so focused on what God hasn't given us—emotional satisfaction, complete spiritual fulfillment, ceaseless happiness—that we are willing to walk away from what he has given us. And we reveal that we have come to Jesus on our terms, not his.

This is similar to what happens in some marriage relationships when partners walk down the aisle with unrealistic expectations. If you're like me, you've been to a few weddings celebrating marriages that were doomed by assumptions from the very beginning. When people believe their spouse will satisfy all their emotional needs, they are in for disappointment. And for some people it's easy to believe they picked the wrong person to marry, or that the marriage has simply failed on its own. They give up and walk away from a relationship that may have been successful with a different set of expectations.

We look for quick fixes. When our beliefs tell us we have found satisfaction and life merely needs to reflect it, we convince ourselves that things are simpler than they are. We focus on trying to change circumstances that seem to stand between us and the satisfaction we claim should be ours: If only we had enough love, everything would be all right. If only there were no poverty . . . if only we had prayer in schools . . . if only we could turn back the clock . . . as if the complexities of our lives and human behavior could be solved with one simple circumstance.

We believe God owes us. When we believe Jesus must satisfy us, we are likely to develop a warped perspective of what we deserve from God. We might think we deserve to be happy, to have only good gifts; everyone else deserves justice but we deserve mercy. When we don't feel satisfied, we become demanding rather than grateful for God's incredible grace and mercy.

When our society talks about the current generation of young adults, popularly called millennials, one of the words most frequently used is *entitled*. Generational descriptions are always very general and frequently resented, but they tend to reflect many people's experiences and observations. So while many people in this generation do not think or behave as if they are entitled to everything they want (without having to work or sacrifice for it), many others do—and they have made an impression. Frankly, I have experienced this firsthand as a manager, hiring and supervising young people who seemed to believe they were entitled to undeserved and unearned raises and promotions, constant praise, and unreasonable flexibility.

The funny thing is, when older adults complain about this sense of entitlement, we rarely consider why a generation might develop such a characteristic. And, again speaking in a broad generalization, we can blame ourselves. Entitlement is based in expectations. When children grow up receiving whatever they want, hearing others tell them they can do whatever they want to do, and learning they are all above average (something that is statistically impossible), they expect life to unfold for them in a way that's consistent with these experiences. When it doesn't, can we wonder why they complain and whine about having only what we would have loved to have at their age? Our cultural indulgence set them up for expectations life simply can't fulfill.

Something similar happens when we expect Jesus to give us complete satisfaction—we can develop a dangerous sense of spiritual entitlement.

We build our theology around satisfaction. When we believe we're supposed to have satisfaction in our relationship with Christ, or we promise satisfaction to others, we are tempted to justify our claims with trite sayings and empowering verses pulled out of context and placed on bumper stickers, refrigerator magnets, and the wallpaper on our smartphones. Pretty soon we end up with an unsustainable faith we have designed to bolster our feelings of satisfaction or help us deny our longing. We place our hope in formulas and what amount to incantations—platitudes dismissing reality or crumbling in the face of it.

We settle for betrothal. Revelation 19 presents an amazing picture of what the future holds for those who follow Christ. This chapter depicts a marriage feast, a celebration of the official union between the Lamb (Jesus) and his bride (the church, those who have been forgiven and made new by Jesus' sacrifice). Before this celebration can take place, the bride is given new clothes to wear—clothes that symbolize righteousness. That righteousness comes from God himself, and it is required.

Although Christians are forgiven and adopted into God's family, and Jesus' righteousness serves as a substitute for our own, we don't currently possess the righteousness we need to be acceptable as the bride of Christ. We are betrothed to him, promised and pledged to be united with him for eternity. Until we are given that true righteousness after God's judgment, we are not ready—or worthy—to celebrate the wedding. There is a distance between us and God that we don't have the power to overcome. When we insist that this relationship, with its distance, is enough to satisfy us, we are settling for only the promise, not its fulfillment. Like any loving bridegroom, Jesus wants us to look forward to the wedding.

We suppress our appetite for God. When we insist that our experience of God is enough to satisfy us, we may successfully convince ourselves we don't want or need more. But as with people who are dieting and trying to quiet their cravings (or their growling stomachs), this isn't really a matter of satisfaction. It's simply a matter of self-denial. There's nothing to be gained here. Rather than suppressing it, we should cultivate an appetite for deeper understanding, a more intimate connection, and a more confident trust.

We move to Laodicea. In Revelation 3:14-22, Jesus addresses the church in Laodicea. The people in this church were wealthy and comfortable, and Jesus had no words of praise for them. "You are neither cold nor hot. I wish you were either one or the other!" Jesus said. "So, because you are lukewarm—neither hot nor cold—I am about to spit you out of my mouth." This imagery is harsh, and it's shocking to realize Jesus' distaste for this church was based not on wanton sin or blatant rejection of him. After all, they were believers. It was based on their satisfaction with their status before God. Although Jesus saw them as "wretched, pitiful, poor, blind and naked," they believed they were wealthy and didn't need anything more. They wanted the benefits of being associated with God, but they did not want the sacrifice, commitment, or transformation that come from true relationship with him. They rejected the passion of hunger and thirst and held Christ at arm's length. He was not impressed.

We miss the value of suffering. The Bible says a lot about the benefits of suffering—it can be a tool God uses to refine our character, teach us more about himself, help us identify more closely with Christ, and aid us in ministry to others (see Romans 5:3-5; 2 Corinthians 1:3-4; 1 Peter 4:12-29). God is not sadistic; he empathizes and comforts us when we're in pain. Yet he does not waste our hardships, and our experiences confirm that suffering can be fertile ground for growth. When we are looking only for satisfaction, we will do almost anything to avoid suffering or to end it. So often we give people the understanding that if they're not satisfied or feeling happy, or they're suffering in some other way, something is *wrong* with their relationship with God. It's possible that relationship has never been more right.

We get sick. I have written and spoken extensively on the topic of mental illness and the church's relationship to mental health problems (see my book *Troubled Minds: Mental Illness and the Church's Mission*). I am adamant that the church recognize that mental illness is not simply a spiritual problem. Every form of mental illness is a complex kind of disorder, and any mental health crisis can have multiple contributing causes—and most require at least some degree of medically based treatment. At the same time, I cannot discount the important impact our spiritual health has on our mental health (and vice versa). And our thoughts themselves have powerful influence on the way our brains function. In some cases—especially with the most common forms of mental illness, like depression and anxiety disorders—our thoughts and beliefs can literally make us sick. And when we are living with emotional or mental dysfunction, our beliefs certainly can keep us from getting better. So can our habits.

Disappointment isn't good for us. As one doctor wrote,

> People who are disappointed are at greater risk of physical or emotional difficulties, or both. Such individuals appear to have a greater frequency of headaches, gastrointestinal difficulties, moist palms, and over-perspiration than those scoring low on this scale. For some, being very disappointed for prolonged periods of time can lead to chronic stress problems.
>
> Disappointment results from thoughts and expectations being out of line with reality. Your expectations and hopes for others may be too high for the situation at hand. Even if you think your expectations are appropriate and realistic, they may not be realistic at all. One solution is to change your expectations to more realistic levels.

Obviously, disappointment is part of life for everyone. However, it does not have to be a long-term or frequent state of mind. One reason disappointment hurts us is because it is a form of dissonance— a conflict between our internal expectations and external reality. When we hold on to unrealistic expectations, or persist in demanding that our experience of life be something it's not, we position ourselves for ongoing dissonance and a sense of conflict with our own lives as they unfold.

When we are desperately seeking satisfaction, and we believe God is holding out on us, we can find ourselves walking down the road to bitterness and even despair. When our expectations are misguided, disappointment is likely. And this is a destructive place to dwell. The demand for satisfaction puts us at risk. It sets us up for a kind of dissonance that is difficult to resolve without changing what we expect from our lives or from God.

SEEKING SATISFACTION HURTS OTHERS

We aren't the only ones who are hurt by our misunderstanding of what is available to us in this life. We hurt other people too, particularly when we give them the impression that being unsatisfied is a sign that something is wrong with their faith.

We give false hope. When we proclaim the message of satisfaction to others, we set them up to come to Jesus with false expectations. We do the world a disservice when we teach, or even suggest, that simply knowing Jesus or following God's ways of living brings total and immediate satisfaction. Our unhealthy appetites don't necessarily go away, and even our healthy desires will not be truly and fully met. And when Jesus and his people don't deliver on the promise, many people give up on faith, deciding it "doesn't work."

In my lifetime of growing up in the church, reaching out to others, and working in Christian media, I have seen many people come to the church, and to Jesus, in moments of crisis. For some, these moments were the greatest fulcrums in their lives, the point on which everything turned. Usually not instantly, but over time, Jesus transformed them. And as they changed, so did their circumstances and the patterns that had defined their lives.

But for other people, those moments of surrender didn't last. As soon as the crisis resolved or the sorrow passed, they went back to their old ways. Or when they realized Christ actually wanted to change them, rather than simply fix their problems, they walked away. They hadn't come to Jesus with true surrender in mind—they had come for quick solutions. And Jesus is not interested in fixing our problems while ignoring their source. We encourage this kind of shallow approach to Christ when we promise he will cheerfully make our lives what we want them to be, like a fairy godmother.

We limit transformation. When we tell people that the world doesn't satisfy but Christ does, we encourage them to come to him with the same needs they looked to the world to meet, expecting him to make them go away or to soothe them. We ask people to simply transfer their desire for comfort, self-satisfaction, or emotional numbness to Jesus, and we create the expectation that if they do so, Jesus will give them what they think they want—or will make sure they never feel anything overwhelming. But we must approach Christ differently, ready to be transformed and to live for his kingdom, not our good feelings. We must be ready for him to redeem our desires, not simply satiate them.

We stigmatize hunger. Telling people their relationship with Jesus will bring satisfaction feeds a sense of stigma and marginalization attached to unsatisfaction. Instead of seeing hunger as a good thing to be directed at the right food source, we give the impression that hunger is a sign of weak faith. We blame people for their suffering or their lack of satisfaction, and we send them looking for remedies to bolster their faith and make themselves feel better when God may be drawing them toward an uncomfortable deepening of relationship. We force people to choose between two false options when something goes wrong in their lives: either they're unacceptable to God or Christianity is bunk.

We encourage hypocrisy. If being unsatisfied is a sign of weak faith or God's rejection, who wants to admit to it? Not many people who want to be part of the church. So people walk around feeling the abyss inside them yet unwilling to acknowledge it—perhaps even to themselves. They close off the pathway to that yawning emptiness, preventing the ministry of others from touching it and not inviting God into it. As with all hypocrisy, it threatens to eat them alive.

We make obviously false promises. When we make claims we can't support, we can actually drive people further away from God. In a blog post titled "There Is No God-Shaped Hole," one atheist writer cites a survey of religious and nonreligious people that compared, among other things, their level of life satisfaction and emotional well-being. According to him, the study found that people who are confident in their beliefs (strong believers or strong non-believers) are the most satisfied with their lives, with no significant difference between them. As this writer saw it, such a study is evidence that the claims of Christianity are false. Now, I would contend that he is refuting a false claim: "that belief in God fills an emotional void that can't be quenched by other means." But I can't blame him for attacking it or viewing it as a tenet of Christian belief; I've heard it more times than I can count. When we make claims like this, we set ourselves up to be discredited and give people more reason not to believe.

Perhaps one reason we so easily embrace the idea that being in relationship with Jesus should completely satisfy our emotional and spiritual needs here and now is because we are afraid of the alternative. But dissatisfaction is not the only other option. This book is about another option: unsatisfaction. It's a better way to live, and it's not the same as being dissatisfied.

DISSATISFACTION IS NOT OUR ONLY CHOICE

Dissatisfaction is a word that brings to mind some pretty unappealing characters: Veruca Salt, the spoiled and demanding girl in *Charlie and the Chocolate Factory*; Harry Potter's cousin Dudley

Dursley, who threatened a tantrum on his eleventh birthday because he received thirty-six birthday gifts instead of thirty-eight; Thorin Oakenshield, the exiled dwarf king in *The Hobbit*, who lived to regain his ancestral wealth and enlisted the help of others, only to turn on them and hoard his treasure once he had it.

For dissatisfied people, no amount is enough. No thing is adequate. No person is acceptable. Everything falls short because dissatisfied people either expect too much or simply refuse to be pleased. Their orientation toward the world is either insatiable consumption or a permanent and cynical emotional closure brought on by chronic disappointment. Dissatisfaction is an active—sometimes even purposeful—absence, rejection, or refusal of satisfaction in a context where satisfaction is expected. It breeds discontentment, contempt, and a feeling of emptiness. And it is miserable.

But while it might be easy to assume dissatisfaction is our only alternative to seeking satisfaction, it's not. What I advocate in this book is unsatisfaction. The two are different. And in a context where satisfaction is not expected—for now—we can instead choose unsatisfaction.

While dissatisfaction implies either rejection or frustrated pursuit of satisfaction, unsatisfaction is something more like acceptance combined with anticipation. It is acknowledgment of desire without the demand that it be satisfied—a kind of openness that doesn't ask for closure. It is desire that can live with deferral, an embrace of the God-shaped vacuum in us and a commitment to stop trying to make it full, a healthy hunger that is content to wait for the feast.

I love both vegetables and salty foods, and as far back as I remember, I've had a weakness for pickles and olives. When I was a child, someone in our church gave me a giant jar of olives as a birthday gift, reflecting the church's familiarity with my habit of clearing out half the ingredients on the relish tray at every potluck.

I did the same thing at my grandma's house when we gathered with family for holidays. Before the meal was served, my mouth watered at the sight of Grandma's homemade pickles, those succulent olives, and the lovely fresh veggies sitting out with other hors d'oeuvres. I would camp out next to the appetizers and enjoy. Unfortunately, by the time the actual meal was served, sometimes I was too full to really enjoy it.

Unsatisfaction is like having a good appetite on Thanksgiving Day, enjoying the warm aromas from the oven and peeking underneath the foil covering Grandma's succulent pies. Looking forward to a delicious feast with loved ones, you know your hunger will be satisfied and the food will taste great because you haven't filled yourself in the meantime. Can you imagine deciding you can't live with this kind of temporary unsatisfaction and eating Cheetos all day (or filling up on olives) or simply convincing yourself you aren't hungry anymore? You'd miss out on what you really wanted.

Our culture is unaccustomed to being okay with unsatisfaction. When we feel desires, we demand that they be sated. When we feel needs, we take for granted that something is available to either meet the need or temporarily numb the feeling. When we aren't satisfied, we typically become dissatisfied and either deify or vilify the objects of our desire—or desire itself. This phenomenon is not unique to our own culture or times. Religions have always sought to manage or harness human desire. Accepting unsatisfaction simply does not come naturally to humans because we were made for a world with no disruption between our good desires and their good objects.

But we don't live in that world now, and disruption is background noise from the day we're born. In the words of nineteenth-century writer and minister George MacDonald,

When most oppressed, when most weary of life, as our un-belief would phrase it, let us bethink ourselves that it is in truth the inroad and presence of death we are weary of. When most inclined to sleep, let us rouse ourselves to live. Of all things let us avoid the false refuge of a weary collapse, a hopeless yielding to things as they are. It is the life in us that is discontented; we need more of what is discontented, not more of the cause of its discontent.

We live on the rough side of a gap between our current reality and our ultimate desires. Dissatisfaction expects someone or some-thing to close that gap, then complains and grows frustrated when it doesn't happen. Unsatisfaction knows how to live with the gap, aware that nothing within our grasp will close it. Unsatisfaction keeps the gap in view, allowing it to produce a healthy sense of longing and a motivation. After all, having desires isn't the problem; it's the direction those desires point us, the shape they take, and what we do with those desires, that can be a problem.

If we ask God to remove our desires or satisfy them with what lies within our reach, even spiritually speaking, we tragically mis-understand his intentions for us. "He who began a good work in you will carry it on to completion until the day of Christ Jesus," Paul wrote (Philippians 1:6). God's work in us continues, and it includes transformation of our desires—not their removal. We are not called to be dissatisfied, but we are called to be unsatisfied.

SUSTAINABLE FAITH

Perhaps this is a good place to acknowledge that half of my profes-sional life is devoted to my work as a life and leadership coach. I don't know for sure what image comes to mind when you think of life coaches or leadership coaches, but I recognize that what I'm saying in this chapter (and this book) may sound a little funny coming from a coach. After all, some coaches claim to have easy keys that will unlock any door in your life; many promise a packaged set of steps to satisfaction.

Unfortunately, such coaches are marketing themselves by (probably unintentionally) promising more than they can really deliver. I really believe in coaching and love working with people through the coaching process. I've seen people utterly change because of their experience working with a good coach. But no change comes without a lot of courageous work. No outrageous soul-deep transformation comes without divine work. And no one, no matter how skilled or wise, has the key to complete and lasting fulfillment in a disappointing world. I believe coaching can offer tremendous growth, build internal strength, and lead to a new, more productive perspective. It really can be a catalyst that helps you change your life. But that doesn't mean it will solve everything, give you all the answers, or make your life just the way you want it. That doesn't mean it will make your desires go away or help you find complete harmony with a world filled with violence, viruses, and vicious people. A good, honest coach must be comfortable with helping clients move toward fulfillment, purpose, and courage while still living unsatisfied. That's the kind of coach I am.

While we're here, in this corrupt place, we will never have the truly safe, completely comfortable, consistently happy life we want. Even if we achieve the very best life we could possibly enjoy on this earth, we would still have so much less than what God offers us. Our longings are not meant to drive us toward satisfaction in this life. They're meant to create longing for Christ and what he offers and drive us to him.

This book is really about sustainable faith—faith that can stand in the reality of this world, that can coexist with unsatisfaction and acknowledgment that all is not right with the world and with us.

Blessings of the Unsatisfied Life:
THE BLESSING OF PERSPECTIVE

While we live in this world, bound by time and its byproducts death and decay, unsatisfaction can help us keep an eternal perspective. Generally, satisfied people have little motivation to change their point of view. But unsatisfied people go looking for answers, for hope, for something better on the horizon. And unsatisfaction can lead us to find that "something better" in things that will last forever.

I've never been a big shopper. Perhaps this is partly because I grew up in a family that never had money to spare; recreational shopping was not part of my experience. And when I hung out with friends at the mall as a teenager, or went shopping with girls who had money to burn, it wasn't much fun. In fact, I didn't like the way it heightened my longing for what was out of my reach. I also hated the sense of overstimulation—the constant marketing appeals, the noise, the competition for my attention.

I still don't like those feelings, even though I no longer live in poverty. So you won't see me blowing my budget at the mall or browsing the racks for things I don't need. But thanks to online shopping, I finally understand the allure of acquisition. I have found a form of shopping that is tailor-made for busy introverts. In fact, if you were to spy on me in my home (and I sincerely hope you don't) for long enough, you would see me make impulse purchases for things I don't need and, sometimes, can't really afford. I have discovered the thrill of buying something new, and I have discovered the transient nature of that thrill. Despite all I know and believe, I sometimes push that "Add to Cart" button under the unspoken conviction that one more purchase will be enough to pacify my longings and give me lasting happiness.

But it's never enough. And it never will be.

I am not alone in chasing after the next big enhancement to my life. And it's not just material goods that can catch my eye toward satisfaction. I have always been afflicted by wanderlust (I think there's a genetic component); I love to go to new places and see new things. While financial realities keep me from fulfilling my most alluring travel dreams, I have made it to a few other countries and to forty-six of the fifty United States of America (coming your way, Idaho, Mississippi, North Dakota, and West Virginia!), and these adventures have been enough to put to rest any question of whether these experiences are worth living for. I still find pleasure in going to new places, and I plan to continue traveling as much as I can. But if I were counting on my collection of experiences to make my life worth living, I would be sorely disappointed. Our circumstances just don't hold that power. No life experience will deeply and permanently satisfy us. We need to keep our eyes on what is truly permanent.

When we feel satisfied, or we believe we're supposed to, it's easy to convince ourselves that life as we know it—or what we can make of it—is good enough. With complacency, we invest our best in things that will be taken from us, either at the moment of death or in an earlier moment of grief. We may completely lose sight of the realm "where moths and vermin do not destroy, and where thieves do not break in and steal" (Matthew 6:20).

On the other hand, when we acknowledge we are unsatisfied in a world where death is certain and life can be treated like a cheap commodity, we are far more likely to seek true answers in the realm we can't see. We have a proper foundation for viewing this world through the illuminating lens of God's bigger perspective. We can see just a glimpse of our world as God views it—and feel a bit of his longing for us.

EXERCISES

- Take some time to describe a situation in your life, either on paper or in conversation with a friend. Then consider how that same situation might look different from God's perspective. Speculate on this and try to reframe this small piece of your story from an entirely different point of view. See how this larger perspective changes your own.

- Consider whether you are investing your best in things that will be taken from you, either in death or during your lifetime. Are you devoted to your own comfort, physical appearance, or sense of importance? Consider how your life might be different if you were to redirect that energy toward things that will last forever: sharing the good news of grace and forgiveness through Christ, serving others in Jesus' name, reading and studying the word of God.

- Read and meditate on Psalm 39:4-5 and Isaiah 55:8-11. Ask God to instill in you a sense of how small and short your life on earth is compared to eternity. Thank him for the opportunity to begin living for eternity here and now.

Curses
and Blessings

❧

An important element to living with sustainable faith, to being expectantly unsatisfied, is understanding that life as we experience it is under curse. Praise God that the curse is temporary, and we are right to rejoice in this. But while it lasts, we are also right to grieve it. Living with the consequences of sin is supposed to hurt, and it does! The curse on humanity hurts Jesus' followers as much as it hurts anyone. Before we focus on the blessings that come with living unsatisfied, it's important to acknowledge this is not because of God's design—it's because of what we have chosen.

I often feel baffled when I hear Christians blame God for what humans have done. I don't mean that to be an insensitive statement—I'm familiar with the rage, frustration, and grief that follow tragic circumstances. But anyone who ascribes to Christian theology ought to know better than to expect God to regularly overpower human free will or reverse the natural laws he set to govern our world in order to help us avoid the natural consequences of behavior that breaks his moral laws—whether our behavior or someone else's.

When we cry, "How could God let this happen?" we're usually shaking our fists at the choices other people, or maybe we ourselves, have made in response to the freedom God has granted. Our God, whose ways are higher than ours, has given us the freedom to choose him and to choose how we will live. Many of us cherish this freedom for ourselves and resent it on behalf of others. Our ancestors chose to reject God, and all humanity was cursed, along with the world we live in. Each person born since has affirmed that sinful nature and shared in the consequences of rebellion. We can rail against it all we like, but we live under a curse of our own making and maintenance, and we lack the capacity to lift it.

The only one able to lift sin's curse is God, and he himself has satisfied his own requirements for its end through multiple layers of sacrifice—first taking on the limitations of being human; then living a perfectly sinless life while facing all the same temptations you and I do; then allowing humans to viciously kill him; then suffering the indignity of death, the punishment for sin; then preceding us in resurrection. Yet while the price has been paid, in his grace and wisdom, and for his glory, God continues to allow human history to unfold. Those of us who have been set free from slavery to sin find ourselves still living with the consequences of sin, while entrusted with carrying God's Spirit within us and representing his presence on earth.

ACKNOWLEDGE THE CURSE

The Disney movie *Pirates of the Caribbean* contains a striking illustration of the curse we live under. The movie focuses on *The Black Pearl*, a pirate ship whose crew is condemned to sail under a curse of living death. Stolen Aztec gold came at a very high price: the thieves were dead many times over, but they had not lost their lives. Neither had they lost their appetites. Until the curse was lifted by a blood sacrifice, they would eat and pour drink down their throats, but they could not enjoy the taste and would never be satisfied. They longed for true death; this living death was unbearable.

For people who are, as Paul puts it, "dead in your transgressions and sins" (Ephesians 2:1), living under a curse of our own, this is an apt picture. People need the intervention of God, who "made us alive with Christ" (Ephesians 2:5). And while we are dead, we can pour all manner of things into our souls in the hope of either bringing us to life or killing us—but they all flow right through us.

For those who are alive in Christ, it can be tempting for us to focus so much on the blessings we have in Christ that we forget we still must live with the curse as well. Sometimes we live as if we believe that for Christians God casts a special kind of magic over the things we enjoy in this world, and that our experience with the good things in life should be superior to what others receive. This is wrong! Why would God want us to be satisfied with a world full of shadows of the real thing? Just because my family is Christian doesn't mean they have the power to make me feel complete. Just because my house and car are purchased with funds I earned in honest work as a follower of Christ doesn't mean they will make me truly happy. And just because my church is full of people Jesus has forgiven doesn't mean I can find truly, completely fulfilling community there. God did not make us to be satisfied by these things.

Ignoring this reality can keep us in pursuit of satisfaction, with our heads down, so we miss the best parts of life. And it can drive some to despair. It's far better to acknowledge the curse, grieve its effects even while we enjoy God's blessings, and long for its end, as our patient God does.

THE CURSE BETWEEN US

My husband, Trevor, and I met in college in Illinois, and we went on our first date in March of my sophomore year, his senior year. We continued dating over the next couple of months, and we "defined the relationship" at about the same time he was graduating and moving back to his home state of Colorado, where he would work and attend seminary.

I still had two years of college ahead of me, and when the new school year started we found ourselves living one thousand miles apart, with this growing relationship that increasingly made us long to be together. For a year and a half, we saw each other as much as we could but felt more and more as if one of us was in the wrong place.

Finally, when our relationship progressed to the point where we were both getting serious about marriage, Trevor quit his job, put his seminary education on hold, and moved back to Illinois. At first he didn't have a job or a place to live, so he stayed with a friend who had his own dorm room on campus. Trevor is a very tall man and hard to miss, so I'm not sure whether people thought he hadn't graduated after all or just spent a lot of time with his friend, but somehow he was able to get away with an extended stay. Then, after he found a job and moved in with some friends who shared a house in the area, he became a legitimate resident of the state. Not long after that, we got engaged.

The distance between us didn't keep us from falling in love, but it did cause us grief. And the more deeply we loved each other, the more that distance hurt. Eventually it became unacceptable, and it made Trevor turn his life upside down and move halfway across the country with no job and no home. We will do desperate things to be with the ones we love. I can only imagine what we would do now, after twenty-three years of marriage, if that kind of distance threatened to come between us for a long time.

Similarly, you could say we're in a long-distance relationship with God. We have the curse between us—despite our status as forgiven people, we cannot yet stand in God's actual presence. We cannot bridge the distance between us and God. Christ himself has become that bridge, so we can be friends with God, spiritually reconciled to him. But we cannot live where he lives, cannot understand the world as he does, cannot achieve unimpaired intimacy with him for now. That distance hurts, as it should. And ironically, the closer we grow to him, the less satisfied we are by that relationship and the more frustrated we are by the distance between us.

Similarly, the more deeply we know God, the more uncomfortable we become in this world where righteousness rarely rules the day. The more the Holy Spirit produces his fruit in us (Galatians 5:22-23), the more we struggle to feel at home here. "This memory of Eden haunts us all," Sting sang in his song "Desert Rose." We are indeed haunted not just by what was, but, increasingly as our faith grows, by what will be.

THE IMPORTANCE OF EXPECTATIONS

In the light of this curse on humanity, it's wise to have realistic expectations for what life will offer. We greatly compound our pain and invite disappointment when we expect it to deliver a pervasive and persistent happiness and fulfillment that it won't. In fact, we may just spend our lives driving hard after something we can't achieve—and missing out on what we actually can.

At least one scientific study has determined that the key to happiness in life is low expectations. Researchers at University College London found that when people made a series of decisions resulting in small wins and losses, their happiness with the experience was dependent not on their circumstances but on how their circumstances compared with their expectations. The researchers even created a mathematical equation to reflect their findings, illustrating how strongly happiness is dependent on what we expect. It makes sense: if your expectations are low, you have a greater chance of being surprised by something better than you expect, instead of the other way around.

Of course, our emotional lives are more complex than any mathematical formula, and applying this equation as a wholesale approach to life is likely to backfire. After all, if you set low expectations for your children and other people you lead, they're just as likely to meet those expectations as to exceed them. If you ensure that your expectations are always low enough that you won't experience any disappointment, you won't experience any anticipation either. In fact, you're likely to join the ranks of the world's most pessimistic people—not exactly a recipe for happiness.

But there is much to be said for *realistic* expectations, based in what is true about the world and about you. When we have false expectations—life should be easy, I'm exceptional, life should be nothing but pleasure, I should be happy all the time, God will spare me from pain—we are sure to be disappointed, probably repeatedly. We are almost certain to grow frustrated and angry and to find ourselves wondering why the rest of the world has betrayed us when the world does not have the capacity to offer what we demand of it.

Holiday celebrations are typically stuffed with expectations, and the more people are involved, the less likely those expectations will be met. This year, we're hosting my family for Thanksgiving. My parents, one of my sisters and her family, and my nephew and his wife will join us, along with at least one guest from among another nephew's college friends. I have no idea of everything these folks will expect when they arrive, but I think it's safe to say a big roasted turkey will be involved. I've got that one covered. I think most people will also anticipate playing some games, since previous holidays have set a clear precedent. And because my husband and I want to play games too, we've made sure everyone knows ahead of time that our Thanksgiving meal is a team effort. Everyone has signed up to prepare some food or clean up the kitchen after we eat. This way, all our guests (and our own teenagers) will show up with realistic expectations—and, I hope, will not be disappointed or surprised to find others expecting them to arrive with potatoes in hand.

Sometimes false expectations are rooted in our perceptions of what other people experience, shaped by pictures on social media and smiling faces at church. They project their idealized images toward us and we project the same back at them, reinforcing each other's faulty assumptions about what life can and should be. When we ascribe to the belief that life in relationship with God will completely satisfy all our needs and desires here and now, we put ourselves under a lot of pressure to appear as if our lives conform to this standard. And when we put up that façade, we become hypocrites who put social pressure on others to exercise the same kind of hypocrisy.

This is no benign social game; living without integrity never is. And when we perpetuate this kind of falsehood, we set up ourselves and others to be devastated by life's serious challenges, the kind we haven't made room for in our tightly controlled theology. When people find themselves confronting mental health crises, addiction in their families, dissolving marriages, chronic pain and disease, relentless misfortune, underemployment, breathtaking loss, or a general sense of disappointment, they are forced to recognize their lives are not living up to expectation. If their theology and the images of people around them have given them reason to expect that God completely satisfies those he really loves and protects them from the consequences of human rebellion, they may not have a framework for understanding their personal tragedies as anything other than God's rejection or even attack. They may be tempted to give up on God, give up on life, or simply consider themselves outside the ranks of the lovable.

I love the way John closed the book of Revelation, his accounting of "what must soon take place" (Revelation 1:1), given to him by the risen and glorified Christ. After describing fantastic visions and events that must have been overwhelming, and which he must have struggled to understand, I can imagine him nearly speechless. After catching a glimpse of God's glory and a curseless new heaven and new earth, he must have ached with desire to be there. In response to Jesus' promise "I am coming soon," John offered a simple expression of longing and hope: "Amen. Come, Lord Jesus" (Revelation 22:20). I echo his longing and his expression of unsatisfaction: Come, Lord Jesus. There is no way I will be truly satisfied when I live in a place where I can't see your face.

Remember, this curse is meant to hurt. Leaving the garden was for our own good—it was also the greatest tragedy in human history. It's hard to live this way. The distance between us and God is a consequence of rebellion against our Creator. But there's good news here too. God uses our suffering to shape us (James 1:2-4) and relentlessly does good in all situations and under all circumstances (Romans 8:28-29), including in our lack of satisfaction—which is not only a curse but also a blessing.

BLESSINGS OF THE UNSATISFIED

Sin's curse on this world is not the end of the story—not even close. Nor is it the whole truth about the human condition. We live in a dark world where light is never quenched, a dry place where beauty and truth keep coming up through the cracks. Our rebellion against God was not the end of God's affection for us; it was an apt beginning for his unpredictable and unflinching displays of generosity, a contrasting background that highlights just how far his love is willing to go. Yes, God allows us to experience the consequences of rebellion—and he stepped out of the limitless realm to let the very worst of those consequences fall on his own head. He knows the truth about us better than we do, and he never walks away from us. Although we are deeply flawed, we are deeply loved. While we cannot save ourselves, we can accept his rescue. We can see grace intervening all around us. We can see the mark of God's nature in every face. No one is ever a hopeless case. And redemption happens all the time.

This is the flip side of curse: blessing. And here's my basic definition of blessing: good things intentionally given. Let's explore this definition further. What does it mean to say God blesses us?

First, blessing is a natural outcome of obeying God, accepting rather than rejecting him—even if the blessing doesn't feel good at the time. God pronounces good things and offers them to us for our choosing, in contrast to the ramifications of disobedience. Before they entered the Promised Land, Moses explained to God's people the choices that lay before them: "This day I call the heavens and the earth as witnesses against you that I have set before you life and death, blessings and curses," he said. "Now choose life," he pleaded, "so that you and your children may live and that you may love the LORD your God, listen to his voice, and hold fast to him" (Deuteronomy 30:19-20). Like Moses, God wanted his people to choose blessing. And he wants us to make the same choice, even if blessing doesn't always look the way we think it should. You could say "blessed" is humanity's natural state (in our original condition) without the interference of sin, the same way the sun is always shining, even when cloud cover makes it appear to be hiding. At the end of time, when the curse is lifted completely, blessing will again be apparent without hindrance or obstruction (Revelation 21–22). This is the general concept of blessing and one aspect of its definition. But this isn't all I mean when I refer to God's blessing.

The second aspect of blessing, beyond what is generally available when we obey God, comes when God offers targeted and gratuitous blessing that mitigates the effects of curse, like rays of sunshine that break through the clouds on an overcast day. Easton's Bible dictionary tells us, "God blesses his people when he bestows on them some gift temporal or spiritual." William E. Brown calls blessing "a state of happiness and recognized favor with God." According to *Strong's Concordance* and *HELPS Word-Studies*, the Greek word *makarios*, usually translated "blessed" in the Bible, "describes a believer in *enviable* ('fortunate') position from receiving *God's provisions (favor)*—which (literally) *extend* ('make long, large') His grace (benefits). This happens with receiving (obeying) the Lord's inbirthings of faith." God's blessings aren't just general; they're also specific. And God is so gracious, he offers these blessings to people who have not earned them through obedience. In fact, he offers righteousness itself—purchased through his own sacrifice—to us as the ultimate blessing.

In his infinite grace and compassion, God has not abandoned us to our chosen fate. He is constantly doing the work of redemption, whether in paying for our lives with his own, reinventing our dreams and desires, or changing dead ends into fresh starts. God intentionally gives good things to us, both as rewards for choosing his way and as gifts that simply express his character and his love for us. These good things are blessings. And some of these blessings come in funny wrappings, like the wrapping of unsatisfaction. He blesses us not only despite our rebellion but sometimes through its consequences. This is great news! Unsatisfaction is not only a symptom of curse; it's also a blessing.

THE UPSIDE-DOWN SERMON

Recorded in Matthew 5–7 is the most famous of Jesus' sermons, known as the Sermon on the Mount because, according to Matthew 5:1, it was delivered on a mountainside. I think we should consider giving it a more auspicious title, such as the Bombshell Sermon, the Upside-Down Sermon, or the Sermon That Ruined Religion. After all, this was a sermon in which Jesus took a lot of closely held legalistic assumptions that made people feel they were fulfilling God's law, turned them upside down, and shook them until they fell apart. He contradicted the system of religion that ruled his listeners' lives at the time—basically the system human nature is always constructing around its own perceived strengths. He told his audience their thoughts and intentions were just as important as their actions. He told them to offer the other side of their faces to people who wanted to hurt them. He told them to love their enemies, to pray and fast and practice generosity in secret, and to save as much wealth as they could—in heaven, not on earth. He told them to look at their own sin before correcting others. And before he said any of it, he completely overturned common religious assumptions about what it looks like to be blessed by God.

The opening statements of Jesus' sermon, in Matthew 5:3-12, are commonly known as the Beatitudes. These are statements of blessing, announcing God's favor and good things intentionally given to specific kinds of people. Then, as now, people were commonly thought to be blessed if they enjoyed comfortable circumstances and got what they wished for—and particularly if they had reason to be self-satisfied in their piety. But Jesus told a different story. Essentially, he told his congregation that the ones who are truly in enviable position are spiritually needy, mourning, meek, hungry and thirsty for righteousness, merciful, pure-hearted, peacemaking, persecuted, and mistreated because of loyalty to Christ. As Lawrence O. Richards wrote, "These surprising statements of blessing underline the difference between human values and God's and call us to view life and success God's way."

The word translated as "blessed" in most versions of these verses is *makarios*, the same word mentioned earlier that refers to a position made enviable by God's favor. It's important to note that this blessing is positional, not emotional. As W. C. Allen points out, the language used in the Beatitudes "describes a state not of inner feeling on the part of those to whom it is applied, but of blessedness from an ideal point of view in the judgment of others." There is no expectation that people who mourn feel happy, that people who are poor in spirit feel rich, that people who hunger and thirst for right-eousness feel satisfied. In fact, while these verses speak of blessing in the present tense, they speak of comfort, fullness, and inheritance as future realities. A simplistic parallel is the position of a child with a broken bike, desperately wishing someone would fix it, who learns she'll be getting a brand-new bike (currently hidden in the garage) for Christmas. She may not feel blessed, because she doesn't have it yet, but she is because it has her name on it.

In reading these verses about those who may not feel blessed but are, we discover that God blesses people who acutely feel the ef-fects of human corruption, who are willing to live a countercultural life, who are living for a world beyond this one. In Matthew 5:6 we see that God blesses a specific group of people with a promise of satisfaction, and it's not the ones who claim to have all they need now; it's those who continue to hunger and thirst for righteousness.

As I discussed in chapter one, this verse pronounces blessing on people who are longing not only to be righteous but also to see God's righteousness reign. They are longing for the better world we were all made for—a longing that will not be satisfied in this life. Jesus did not proclaim that these people are blessed because they can direct their longing toward a relationship with him and thus receive satisfaction here and now. He did not trivialize their hunger and thirst just as he did not trivialize the pain of mourning or the ongoing work of peacemaking and being pure in heart. Coming into right relationship with God does not dismiss the need for these attitudes and actions. These are active, lifelong conditions

God sees and will reward. Jesus declared we are in an enviable position not when we are fully satisfied in him but when we stay hungry and thirsty—desperate for his kingdom, desiring not the immediate satisfaction of our appetites but that God be honored and obeyed in our hearts and everywhere. This is an appetite God created in us and wants to satisfy. As Albert Barnes wrote,

> They shall be satisfied as a hungry man is when supplied with food, or a thirsty man when supplied with drink. Those who are perishing for want of righteousness; those who feel that they are lost sinners and strongly desire to be holy, shall be thus satisfied. Never was there a desire to be holy which God was not willing to gratify, and the gospel of Christ has made provision to satisfy all who truly desire to be holy.

But it gets even better. The hunger of unsatisfaction is not only a blessing for the future; it's also a blessing now, in several different ways. And we choose those ways when we embrace a life of unsatisfaction.

Blessings of the Unsatisfied Life:
THE BLESSING OF GOD'S HEARTBEAT

For now, while we long for a better world, unsatisfaction keeps us connected to a world God loves. Selfish creatures that we are, if we were truly satisfied here and now, I'm afraid we would not long for what God longs for. I'm afraid we would give up on a world God has not stopped caring for. Our hearts would not quicken with the approaching sound of perfect justice and full redemption—not only for us, but for the whole earth.

My husband, Trevor, grew up in Colorado, and his family still lives there, most of them in the Denver area. We drive from Chicago to Denver and back at least once a year at Christmastime. Trevor and I met while we were in college in the Chicago area, and in the twenty-five years we have known each other, we have traveled the interstates between Chicago and Denver, and to points in between, more times than we could possibly count. We're very familiar with the route, the landscape, the milestones, and the most convenient stops along the way. Even our kids now recognize repeat visits to specific rest areas and fast-food restaurants.

Because we always have the same purpose and destination for these trips, we don't treat them like leisurely travel or adventures of discovery. We aren't particularly curious about the places we pass in rural Illinois, Iowa, Nebraska, and Colorado. We're just passing through on our way to somewhere else.

It's only our unsatisfied needs that make us stop. We pull over when we have to fill up on gas, use the bathroom, or buy some food. And when we need to stop, we suddenly become very interested in the place we're driving through: Where's the next gas station? Does it look like the kind of place that might have a clean bathroom? What are the options for getting a meal? And once our needs are satisfied, we get back in the car and keep going, still driven by our own needs and desires. We don't spend a lot of time being curious about the people who live there, getting to know them or empathizing with their everyday challenges. If we wanted to really understand any of the places where we stop and the people who live there, we would have to live there ourselves.

This is true on a more existential level as well. The fact that we suffer alongside everyone else is ultimately good for our hearts. If we are to be known by our love (John 13:35), we should welcome unsatisfaction because it can help keep us tender and open toward others. Unsatisfaction reminds us we are sinners at God's mercy, living in and among the consequences of our rebellion, just like everyone else. It enables us to be mission-minded, motivated by love for people we can fully identify with. We long with and for our neighbors in a way we would not if we did not, like them, wish for a better world.

This is part of the appeal of the television show *Undercover Boss*, in which high-level executives go undercover in their own companies, filling the jobs of ordinary workers. They quickly find out what life is like for employees and how things really work in the trenches of their own corporations. The results are, of course, entertaining. They can be funny, sad, poignant, and powerfully enlightening for the bosses. No amount of time in corner offices in executive suites at corporate headquarters could replace the experience of serving as frontline workers. Some of these bosses have come from humble origins and can relate to the people they work alongside in their undercover experiences. For others who have always lived a more privileged life, the experience produces a sense of empathy they would not have picked up anywhere but in the kitchens, warehouses, or storefronts of their own organizations. Until they enter on equal footing and work alongside the people who work for them, they can't truly understand how their policies and decisions affect other people. And confronted with clear evidence that changes are necessary, they care more deeply and personally than they would have cared before.

Can you imagine what we would be like if God insulated us from the effects of sin and suffering in this world? If we could hide out in the spiritual equivalents of corner offices, "rising above" the problems of people around us and enjoying the perks of belonging to Christ? I fear we would not be compassionate people, eager to get our hands dirty on behalf of the rest of humanity.

Satisfied people tend to sit in their satisfaction and to downplay the desperation of those who long for relief. Unsatisfaction motivates us to hold a better vision for ourselves and others. God loves everyone and wants to be in relationship with every human being. God wants us to ache for those who don't know him. He wants us to groan along with all of creation and long for its redemption (Romans 8:19-25). When we feel our own longing for these things, we are connected to God's own heart.

Instead of satisfaction, life with Jesus leads us to a deeper, more righteous kind of unsatisfaction. As we know him more, we become more unsatisfied by what grieves God and hurts people (and the rest of his creation). Instead of satisfying us, he changes our longings to be more like his.

EXERCISES

- Consider some of the difficult things you have been through and how God has used them to make you tender toward other people. Thank God for those circumstances, acknowledging that while they may not have been good, and they certainly weren't satisfying, God has done (and will do) good things through them.

- Ask God, or a wise Christian friend, to show you an area where you have been fruitlessly pursuing satisfaction for yourself. Then ask God how you might instead let that specific sense of unsatisfaction motivate you to care for others. For example, maybe your experience with illness, injury, or physical pain has caused you to relentlessly pursue your own health. Perhaps it can also inspire you to advocate for people who need help in accessing health care.

- Seek out someone at the margins, whose pain or hardship you are tempted to ignore. Ask God to help you see that person the way he does. Then behave accordingly. Perhaps your response will be as simple as making eye contact, saying hello, or calling an overlooked person by name.

How to Live the Unsatisfied Life

So what do we do for now, as we anticipate ultimate satisfaction in unbroken fellowship with God? How do we live a good, unsatisfied life? Is it possible to embrace unsatisfaction and lead a life that's endurable? Absolutely! Intentionally unsatisfied is the best way to live.

I suspect some readers fear an unsatisfied life looks like the one described by the Grinch (played by Jim Carrey) in Ron Howard's 2000 movie *How the Grinch Stole Christmas.* When he's invited to join the Whos in Whoville for an over-the-top Christmas party, he reviews his schedule: "Even if I wanted to go, my schedule wouldn't allow it. Four o'clock, wallow in self-pity. Four-thirty, stare into the abyss. Five o'clock, solve world hunger, tell no one. Five-thirty, Jazzercize. Six-thirty, dinner with me—I can't cancel that again. Seven o'clock, wrestle with my self-loathing. . . . I'm booked. Of course, if I bump the loathing to nine, I could still be done in time to lay in bed, stare at the ceiling, and slip slowly into madness. But what would I wear?"

The Grinch's life is empty. He is dissatisfied, discontented, and disconnected. His sense of meaning is found in nursing old grudges, and his longings have been buried for decades beneath hurt and cynicism. Oh, and his heart is two sizes too small. His capacity for love is severely impaired.

Thankfully, the Grinch's life is not what I have in mind for any of us. An unsatisfied life need not be empty. We can be unsatisfied and live with purpose, meaning, and a sense of fulfillment. Unsatisfied people can enjoy the good things in life and be content with what they have. There is more to being unsatisfied than staring into Pascal's "infinite abyss." In fact, embracing the unsatisfied life with Christ can mean even that abyss is no longer something to fear or avoid.

STARE INTO THE ABYSS

I'm a voracious reader, with a relentless appetite for good literature, and I have two daughters who are the same way. As they've been working their way through the world of teen and young adult fiction, I've sometimes accompanied them, reading the same books they're reading. In recent years, some of the most popular new works in this category have been dystopian novels—stories that feature a world that is far from ideal (in fact, the opposite of utopian perfection), corrupt, and usually unsustainable. Often the characters in these worlds display the best and worst of what humans can be, and they face exaggerated versions of the same problems we deal with in the real world. Typically, God as we know him doesn't enter the picture.

The most famous example is *The Hunger Games* trilogy, which depicts life in the future land of Panem (located where the United States currently exists). A central district, The Capitol, rules and oppresses the people in thirteen surrounding districts and lives in despicable extravagance while the people in the districts are barely surviving. The annual Hunger Games drafts teenagers from the districts, puts them on a reality television show, and requires them to fight to the death.

Another popular series is the *Divergent* trilogy, set in post-apocalyptic Chicago. In this series's society, those in power control the populace by sorting people according to personality tendencies and placing them into five different factions. Each faction focuses on developing one designated virtue. Sixteen-year-olds are required to swear their allegiance to their faction, and any deviation is not tolerated. As you might expect, conflict ensues.

Some Christians express concern about the darkness in these worlds, presumably believing it's better to read about worlds where truly bad things don't happen and people are always rewarded for their good deeds. But Christians should be more willing than anyone to acknowledge what humans are capable of and to consider how dark a world without God's intervention might be—and how imperfect human solutions will always be. After all, in Anne of Green Gables' world, what will possibly make her realize she needs God?

Sadly, many Christians feel that acknowledging our darker impulses is the same as indulging them, that admitting how very hopeless we are on our own is an exercise for people lost in darkness. People who live in this denial are missing out on the full joy of new life in Christ—because they're not willing to acknowledge the full truth about themselves without him.

Staring into the abyss need not be a fearful, despairing experience done without hope. In fact, it may be the first thing you need to do. When people try to deny their sense of unsatisfaction and their longing for what nothing finite can give them, they tend to order their lives around avoiding what they fear. They walk around the abyss, pretending it's not there, while in reality it's dictating their every movement. For people who have convinced themselves that Christians should be satisfied and that living unsatisfied is the same as living an empty life, the idea of acknowledging unsatisfaction may feel like it threatens the foundations of their faith.

But it doesn't! The abyss is a foundational doctrine of our faith. It's an expression of the fact that we need God. We need more of him than we can get in this life. And we don't stop needing him when we live in relationship with him.

I encourage you to look into your own abyss. Start journaling, hire a coach or spiritual director, see a Christian counselor, make an appointment with a pastor, or ask a trusted and wise friend to listen to you. This takes a lot of courage and honesty, and you may need someone to not only support you but also challenge you toward it. Admit that you want more than you can ever receive in this life. Acknowledge what you're missing and what you wish for. Consider how it motivates you. Take those longings before God— not to ask him to remove them, but to be honest before the one who knows better than you how very much you're missing.

RETHINK YOUR CAPACITY

Like the rest of our society's commonly acceptable language, the jargon of medical professionals is full of euphemisms. The patient didn't have a stroke; he had a cerebrovascular accident. She patient didn't die; she simply didn't make it. The treatment wasn't a failure; it had a negative patient outcome. Sometimes these phrases are amusing; sometimes they're compassionate. Sometimes they're painfully unclear when people really need clarity. Among the most potentially offensive is the phrase "not compatible with life," suggesting a very detached survey of circumstances and an emotionless response to a painful conclusion: unless conditions change, death is inevitable. And those conditions can't always change. It simply means something is wrong to the degree that the person cannot survive as things stand—or may already be dead and beyond hope of resuscitation.

Many people respond similarly to the idea that we can't be truly satisfied in this life. They believe living unsatisfied is a condition incompatible with life. And this belief motivates them to resolve the conflict by either changing the offending circumstance to find satisfaction, or convincing themselves they're satisfied when they're not. This misconception produces the kind of desperation that keeps people shopping, eating, drinking, looking for love, chasing fame, and demanding more from God even when they know this still won't produce the satisfaction they're seeking.

But unsatisfaction is something you can live with—we all do, whether we admit to it or not. Regardless of what you may have been conditioned to believe, you can tolerate not being satisfied. In fact, I believe unsatisfied is the very best way to live under the conditions we all have in commom. You don't have to try to make your unsatisfaction go away.

I know this from experience. Years before I understood that my mom had schizophrenia, I knew something had gone wrong with her mind. As a very young adult I was happy, growing, and enjoying life. At the same time I was angry, deeply sad, and powerfully ashamed of what my mother's mental health might say about me. So I packed away my pain, trying to keep it hidden from myself and from everyone I was certain would reject me if they knew.

But God didn't let me stay the way I was. Over time, he gave me courage and opportunity to seek counseling and begin the healing process. Eventually he gave me courage to engage my family in a new way, challenging the conspiracy of self-protection we had built. He helped me understand that this kind of pain doesn't stop, because it's not supposed to. But it can be made beautiful through the power of God's suffering and his remarkably redemptive love.

In the process I have come to realize that God isn't interested in removing my wounds; he's interested in redeeming and using them. I believe God wants me to live at peace with this ongoing undercurrent of sadness, not focus on trying to make it go away. But sadness doesn't have to take over my life. It's something God has used to shape me and make me a little more into the person he wants me to be.

We can and do live without complete satisfaction because we have great hope: in his grace God causes beauty to grow in the soil of sorrow. I grew up a lot when I gave up trying to stop my grieving. I will always grieve for my loss and for what my mom has endured. And I should—that's not something you get over or rationalize away. But I can still live a full and enjoyable life. Like unsatisfaction, healthy grief keeps my heart open and tender. And it can do the same for you. You have the same capacity.

STOP THE CHASE

It's time to stop looking for what you won't find. While working toward a better life and a better world are worthy pursuits, neither requires that you have a truly satisfying life. In fact, this particular chase is likely to distract you from what is better.

When I was growing up, my sister received a kitten as a gift from one of her friends (if you can call someone a friend after she gives you a potentially fertile female cat as a gift). She named the cat Cuddles, and my family gave her a good home. And one day Cuddles rewarded us by giving birth to a litter of eight kittens. Being fans of moderation, our family paid it forward and gave some gifts of our own, keeping two of Cuddles' sons as additions to our own family. I think we must have gotten Cuddles spayed too, because that never happened again.

Like all fun-loving cat owners, we enjoyed the well-worn game Cat Chases the Light. My siblings and I would shine a flashlight on the wall and move it around, watching the cats chase the beam in their determined dance. Every time they thought they had it . . . a good pounce . . . nothing.

This is the image that comes to mind when I think of us chasing satisfaction. We're trying to capture something we think we see—that doesn't exist for us here and now. We make ourselves exhausted and foolish, and we lose sight of what we're actually here for.

Knowing you can and must live without it, you have no need to keep chasing satisfaction. Take the time and energy you've been wasting on this pursuit and apply it toward living with purpose (more on that to come). By all means, keep your eyes on the true source of light—but don't get distracted by trying to capture and consume every glowing beam that comes across your path.

ACCEPT NO SUBSTITUTES

People who follow Christ and live under his grace, who have acknowledged that the world won't satisfy their longings, still face daily temptation to chase satisfaction, not only in their faith but also in what this world has to offer. The funny thing is, when we look through the eyes of God's Spirit, we can see right through the tantalizing promises of products and people. But sometimes we still like to believe that the shiny package really does contain everything we lost just east of Eden.

Like all temptations, this one is far harder to resist when we are weak and vulnerable. And we make ourselves easy targets when we indulge the belief that we can find (and probably deserve) satisfaction in this life. We set ourselves up to believe the next person who comes along and tells us we can't live with longing.

Refuse to accept substitutes for true satisfaction. Don't be fooled and distracted by what this world promises. Some substitutes are obviously a bad idea (such as abusing drugs, engaging in extramarital sex, using pornography, binge drinking). But other, seemingly innocuous things—friendships, family relationships, work, physical fitness, achievement, personal comfort, beautiful things, good works—may be harmful to us if we use them in attempt to dull our unsatisfaction, distract ourselves, or assure ourselves we don't need anything.

When we accept unsatisfaction instead and let go of the illusion that we can make it go away, we strengthen our position. We can more easily see and starve the lust that drives us toward substitutes for God and his good gifts.

REJECT DISSATISFACTION

If we want to live unsatisfied and well, it's important to guard against dissatisfaction, its grudging cousin. And dissatisfaction will make you miserable. Unsatisfied is healthy; dissatisfied is not.

When we become comfortable with the gap between our current reality and our ultimate desires—or at least accept it—we keep our hearts open and eager for God's presence to show itself in the world. This is a completely different posture from what dissatisfaction produces in us: grasping, closed, resistant, dismissive, scoffing.

Dissatisfaction is focused on trying to change circumstances, and complaining about them until they change. Unsatisfaction learns to "get comfortable being uncomfortable," to quote the Navy SEALS—and to enjoy the comforts when they come.

An unsatisfied person can experience joy, relish opportunities to use God-given gifts, build meaningful relationships, invest in personal growth and development, and influence the world with a positive attitude, all without expecting full satisfaction, knowing these things—though they are good—will not cure the condition of any human soul.

A dissatisfied person misses out because he or she is looking to these things to enjoy them not for what they are, but for something they can't provide. Nothing is ever good enough when "good enough" doesn't live on this planet. So guard against dissatisfaction. Watch your expectations, curb complaining, and be careful what (and whom) you try to control.

FUEL UP

When I was a high schooler in the late 1980s, I remember writing an essay for a scholarship application, discussing ways to address the alarming rise in homelessness, a topic of frequent public discussion and concern. I thought I had some pretty fantastic ideas for tackling the problem, although I can't remember much of what I wrote in that essay. But I'm sure my ideas were simplistic, because I do remember that I wrote them based on a one-dimensional understanding of what caused homelessness: poverty and a lack of affordable housing. I didn't understand the strength of the links between homelessness and untreated mental illness, domestic violence, systemic victimization, and a host of other factors, many of which we still haven't figured out. I didn't know how completely addiction can rob a person of self-regard. I didn't know the power of real despair. And I still don't really know all those things for myself.

But I did care. Like most other people, I was unsatisfied by things as they were, and it was not going to be okay with me if we did nothing to help. Unsatisfaction motivated me to think about the issue and advocate (in a very small way) for solutions.

On the other hand, I misunderstood the problem's solvability. If I had been in a position to implement my ideas, I would have been bitterly disappointed to see the results—not because they wouldn't have helped, but because they wouldn't have fixed the underlying problem. A healthy and pervasive state of unsatisfaction could have helped me move beyond my desire to see change to blend it with an understanding that entirely solving the problem was not the only outcome worth fighting for. Just because more affordable housing isn't the entire answer to homelessness doesn't mean it's not worth making more affordable housing available.

This is just one example of the ways people try to change the world, and we do so with all kinds of motivations. Unsatisfaction is a great one. It helps us maintain a vision for how the world can be better. And when we live with the kind of unsatisfaction I'm advocating in this book, it serves as a reality check, helping us avoid the temptation to believe we can carry the world on our shoulders. It can keep us from burnout and disenchantment when our efforts don't make the world the place we want it to be.

Embracing unsatisfaction means acknowledging life should be better than it is, not settling for what we know and convincing ourselves it's all we want. Living comfortably with unsatisfaction can also help us live with the fact that, despite all the good we do, the world is not as it should be. Without expecting magical results, we can call on our unsatisfaction as a source of fuel to help us pursue what's better. We don't have to simply sit back and wait for a better world; we can also actively work toward it while knowing we won't achieve completion.

As you embrace the "now" blessings of unsatisfaction and wait for the "not yet," let your unsatisfaction fuel your reach toward what's better not just on your own behalf, but on behalf of everyone.

CHANGE YOUR APPETITE

While we wait, we can grow in our cravings for what is good and God-given, rather than what we think will make us feel good.

I spent more than twenty years as a vegetarian, so it's a good thing I love vegetables. But unfortunately for my health, as I've already mentioned, I also love salt. It's one of the reasons I've always enjoyed V8 vegetable juice, and I drink it with my breakfast nearly every morning. A few years ago I decided I wanted to try to curb my salt intake (not to address any actual health problem, just because it seemed like a good idea), and I started by buying the low-sodium version of the juice. At first I didn't like it. It tasted much blander than what I was used to. But it didn't take long for me to get used to it and enjoy it. A while later, when my husband accidentally bought regular V8 instead of the low-sodium stuff, I was surprised to realize just how salty it was. I didn't like it as much anymore. In fact, I realized the less-salty version had become my favorite. I had successfully changed my preference. Score one for health! (And I do mean one—I didn't cut back salt on anything else.)

My experience is backed by science. Scientists have determined that our food preferences are almost entirely learned, which makes perfect sense when you consider that most people tend to enjoy foods favored in the culture they grew up in. Our childhood habits aren't the only ones that shape our desires; we can change our preferences as adults. Sometimes these changes are forced on us, like the time when, early in my first pregnancy, I made big batch of a citrus-rice dish and found I couldn't eat more than a few bites before getting sick. After that, every time I looked, smelled, or even thought about that dish I was completely nauseated. I had to throw it all away, and seventeen years later I still feel a little queasy as I remember the taste. But we can also willingly, even intentionally, change our tastes by eating what we want to enjoy, cultivating a taste for it, and learning to savor it.

The same is true outside the realm of food. We can develop tastes for new kinds of relationships, new ways of spending our time, new habits. And apart from our own effort, the Holy Spirit does this kind of work in us when we offer ourselves up as living sacrifices to God, who renews our minds and changes the way we think (Romans 12:2).

People who are chasing satisfaction are most likely to crave what they think will give them what they want—happiness, comfort, pleasure, peace—regardless of whether it is good for them and others. When we choose to live unsatisfied instead, we have an opportunity for intentionality. Rather than desperately grab for what is close at hand or be driven by cravings, we can decide what we want our lives to include: ever-deepening relationship with God, evidence of the Holy Spirit's presence in us, healthy relationships with others, displays of unselfishness, a habit of listening, meaningful work, a positive attitude, acts of service, life-giving words, times of celebration, ease of spirit. We can welcome those things into our lives, disciplining ourselves to engage in them, cultivating a taste for what is good. Over time, as we indulge in what is good, we build a healthy craving for these things, knowing they will not provide ultimate satisfaction but they will help support our transformation into the kind of people we want to be.

BE GRATEFUL

Perhaps no habit is better for us emotionally than gratitude. True gratitude and discontentment are incompatible, so we cannot sincerely thank God for what he has given and done and simultaneously grumble over what we do not have. Unsatisfaction, on the other hand, is completely compatible with gratitude.

In addition to the spiritual benefits, medicine and neuroscience have established that thankfulness is tremendously good for us—particularly for our mental and emotional health. And it doesn't simply put us in a good mood. Gratitude changes the way we function. It's a conscious and intentional process that brings discipline to our thoughts. It changes the chemistry and activity in our brains, and it turns our attention to thought patterns that are good for us rather than destructive. Studies have demonstrated that gratitude decreases depression, envy, frustration, regret, and other emotions that work against us. It can build our resilience and even help us overcome psychological trauma. And when our brains change, so does our sense of purpose and our awareness of why we're here. We can go from focusing on what we don't have to focusing on what we do have and beyond, to what we will have when our longings are fulfilled beyond our wildest imaginings.

When we focus on satisfying ourselves, or on all the ways we have been disappointed in that search, we become more and more focused on what is negative, frustrating, and out of our control. The more we do this, the more we lose sight of what is also true: the positive, the beautiful, the hopeful, the unexpected good, the evidence that God is in control. Expressing gratitude can help expand our perspective to include a more complete version of reality. It's a powerful discipline, and it can engage our thoughts in the right direction, helping us live with unsatisfaction in a healthy way.

English songwriters Matt and Beth Redman have helped many of us express both praise and longing through their popular song "Blessed Be Your Name." After the September 11, 2001, terrorist attacks in the United States, they traveled to various American churches and, during this time, wrote this song of lament, worship, and affirmation of God's sovereignty over all the days of our lives. This song has resonated with so many Christians, who have sung it in recognition of the presence of God—and our need to worship him—every day of our lives.

When I sing this song, I remember the funeral service for my father-in-law, who died in 2006, shortly after his sixty-first birthday. After a long battle with the effects of primary sclerosing cholangitis, a rare disorder that slowly destroys the liver, he was blessed with the life-saving gift of a new liver—only to die weeks later from complications of a failed transplant. In our grief, we gathered to express our sorrow and to acknowledge the blessings of his life. We sang our praise to God, who is worthy of our worship "when the sun's shining" and "on the road marked with suffering." There is no doubt we all longed for a different kind of life, one that doesn't involve losing people we love, yet we could be grateful for God's goodness in our pain.

CULTIVATE UNSATISFACTION

World War I was a monumentally devastating conflict that permanently altered the world's landscape and international relationships. New technology made soldiers more efficient killers than previous generations could have imagined, and somewhere around ten million men were killed and injured in trenches in Europe and on battlefields throughout much of the globe. Ultimately, thirty-two countries were sucked into conflict, and millions of civilians died from injuries, disease, and famine. The conflict is estimated to have killed or injured close to thirty-eight million people altogether.

More than a hundred years later, military experts and historians still argue over the true cause of the war, which was called "the war to end all wars" but which in reality set the stage for World War II and many smaller conflicts, some of which continue today. The best description of the reason for the war is simply that it was a natural consequence of the status quo. Without forethought, empires came to sudden end and new powers emerged. The disruption decimated a generation, both physically and spiritually.

After the war, social upheaval took root throughout the Western world, and young people were particularly disillusioned. In some parts of Europe young women dramatically outnumbered surviving young men. People of all ages deeply distrusted their political leaders. Those who came of age during this time, dubbed the Lost Generation in the United States, keenly felt the drastic changes. To them, everything they had been taught in childhood had been destroyed or revealed to be false. For many, there was little to live for or hope in. So they lived fast and partied hard.

The same political and social realities that gave birth to World War I gave rise to an anarchistic form of artistic expression known as Dadaism. Dadaism was a reaction to social and artistic conventions, with artists seeking to unmask and overthrow conventional ideas not only about art but about society as a whole. It was born out of disillusionment and anti-authoritarianism, an outraged realization that conventional society and its powers had led a blindly submissive world into widespread and senseless slaughter. Marcel Duchamp, among the most iconic of Dada visual artists, produced what he called "readymade" artworks, which amounted to no more than manufactured objects slightly altered and labeled works of art. This was a rebellion against artistic norms. The funny thing is, in reacting against convention these artists produced their own conventions, some of which are now well-established and even taken for granted, entrenched in the artistic establishment. Dadaism simply gave birth to a new status quo.

In its extreme, our search for satisfaction can lead us into the jaws of the same kinds of movements and anti-movements that made our previous century such a deadly one (and which continue to fuel horrific violence in the current one). When we are convinced satisfaction is necessary for life and right around the corner, we set ourselves up to blindly follow self-appointed saviors, join ill-conceived movements, become victims of manipulation and spiritual abuse, and lose our ability to discern right from wrong and wise from foolish. We attach ourselves to the Next Big Answer and the formerly unsatisfied become the new status quo.

Instead, when we recognize the blessings available in unsatisfaction, it begins to make sense that unsatisfied is a condition not to be fought but to be cultivated. Like our Lost Generation predecessors, we have good reasons to be unsatisfied with the status quo and with the prospects for this world with humans at the helm. We should be uncomfortable with spiritual bankruptcy, with the depth of our own relationship with God, with the love we offer others, with the extent to which the fruit of the Spirit displays itself in our lives. We should be disappointed in where our best human efforts have led us. When we admit that our best answers don't resolve our biggest questions, we have good reasons to remain unsatisfied rather than bring ourselves in line with false answers.

Disappointment doesn't have to lead to disillusionment; it can lead to realistic hope in what is to come. When we nurture a healthy unsatisfaction, we stop expecting this world to give us answers it just doesn't have. It encourages us to keep the door open to God's work in us. Holy unsatisfaction is flush with gratitude and with hope in a solution beyond our capabilities and only glimpsed in this life. We draw our hope not from ourselves or our fellow travelers but from its source, who is satisfied only by the work he has done, is doing, and will do in pursuit of his own purposes. Cultivating unsatisfaction can help us keep our hope where it belongs, rather than transfer it from one thing to the next.

Insist on remaining unsatisfied, and let this liberate you! If you are unsatisfied by your life, you probably are not missing out on something. You are well on your way to living in full honesty and alignment with the truth.

LIVE WITH ANTICIPATION

My husband and I are not the "surprise!" type. When we were expecting our first child, we couldn't wait to find out the sex of our baby and tell everyone. So as soon as we possibly could, we were sitting with an ultrasound technician, ready to assign a name and share the news.

We found out she was a girl, and we stopped at the store on the way home from the doctor's office to buy her first outfit. We kept the tags on just in case of technical error, but our hearts went all in. We were full of anticipation to meet the girl who would wear that little cream-colored dress with cherries on it. At home, we hung it in the closet in our second bedroom, and soon, thanks to Grandma-to-be, this unborn child had a whole wardrobe.

We bought a crib, a dresser, and a changing table, and we assembled the crib long before we needed it. We got a car seat, and the good people of our church threw a baby shower that made clear we weren't the only ones ready to welcome this youngster. I remember going into her room before she was born, while I was miserably swollen with her life, to sit in the rocking chair and dream about who she might be. Our anticipation was mixed with a healthy dose of terror, but we couldn't have been more ready to welcome our daughter into the world when she arrived.

Like our daughter's room, an empty place doesn't have to be a place of dread: it can be a place that represents anticipation. The abyss within us is no longer fearsome when we see it as a place of potential, a room that someday will be filled to our satisfaction. Live with anticipation of that day when your longings will be not only met but made irrelevant by the largesse of your Creator.

Don't get me wrong; I'm not talking about an inactive anticipation. If our lives are built around seeking satisfaction, we get ourselves into trouble. But unsatisfaction doesn't mean we simply sit back and wait for a better world. Our anticipation of fulfillment should give us courage and motivation to fully invest ourselves in the opportunities before us. We are called to make something beautiful of this life, in partnership with God. While we abandon the pursuit of complete satisfaction, we can enjoy the blessing of finding meaning, work toward a fulfilling life, appreciate the gift of pleasure, and embrace our calling to contentment—all without insisting our longings be completely satisfied.

After removing satisfaction as the goal of our lives, we can build a life that is unsatisfied and absolutely worth living. Living unsatisfied doesn't mean simply living without satisfaction. There is plenty to include in our lives as well. Each of the following four chapters will focus on one of these important ways to live well while unsatisfied—to fill the empty room with anticipatory furniture, so to speak. To reject both hopelessness and demands and to live with active anticipation of what we know, through faith, is coming. Many people might believe an unsatisfied life means giving up a life of meaning, a sense of fulfillment, enjoyment of pleasure, and contentment. But each of these elements can fit nicely into an unsatisfied life and help us defer the pursuit of satisfaction and get busy with a new and attainable goal.

Blessings of the Unsatisfied Life:
THE BLESSING OF FOCUS

Unsatisfaction can keep us focused on our real reason for hope.

Followers of Christ are not immune to temptation or bad judgment. Like everyone else, we hear the siren songs of materialism, hedonism, and living for our own comfort. And also like everyone else, we are tempted to put our faith in the latest and greatest product, pleasure, prophet, or philosophy. Unlike others, however, we have the gift of the Holy Spirit dwelling in us, guiding us toward—and empowering us for—a way of living that is simultaneously deeper and lighter, more peaceful and more troubled, joyful and marked by sorrow. But we always have a choice, and many of us have chosen to suppress the Holy Spirit's voice in favor of drawing guidance from our most whimsical desires.

It's much easier to believe in what we can see than what we cannot, and so we resist submission to our Creator. We sometimes choose to indulge our self-destructive appetites rather than welcome the Spirit's work in altering and shaping our desires so he can use them to guide us. This is never good for our relationship with God, and it's not good for us personally. Many of the things we consume in pursuit of satisfaction have the ability to consume us in return. They're not all bad or even obvious; good things can become not so good when we build our lives around them. Work, friendships, family life, leisure, helping others, and religious activity all have the capacity to eat us alive when we offer them our souls.

I remember one of my early lessons in the shortcomings of pursuing and getting what I thought I wanted. When I was around ten years old, I was looking through a mail-order catalog and making wishes when I saw something I just had to have. For reasons that are not completely clear to me now, I was seized by a frantic desire to acquire a particular doll. She came with her own stroller, crib, changing table, diapers, bottle, blankets, booties, and change of clothes—all for just thirty dollars! I was astounded at the value. Resources were scarce in my family, but I was a frequent babysitter by then, and this price tag placed the doll within my reach. So I set a goal to save my money until I had enough to order the set.

Even though I was a bit old for baby dolls and not in the habit of playing with them, I was taken with this one, who looked like a large and high-quality doll that a mature young lady like myself could enjoy. As I saved up, I pictured myself playing with the doll, changing her clothes, and pushing the stroller with my beautiful doll inside as other girls looked on in envy. Of course, we lived in the country, on a gravel road, surrounded by cornfields and cattle pastures, so I'm not sure how I thought I would gain an audience of envious peers, but as we all know, dreams don't always make sense.

Finally the day came when I had enough money to pay for the doll and her bountiful trousseau, along with shipping and handling. My parents, whom I remember as somewhat mystified by my fixation, took my money, wrote a check, and helped me place the order. Then I waited the requisite four to six weeks with growing anticipation.

You probably can imagine how my heart leapt at the sight of the package when it arrived—until I noticed the box was much smaller than what I had been expecting. I comforted myself with the knowledge that appearances could be deceiving, so I tore into the box and felt a cold, flat disappointment settle where my anticipation had lived. Everything in the box was cute but cheaply made, childish, and about 80 percent smaller than I had imagined it would be. I remember going back to the catalog to look at the product with more sober eyes and noticing what I hadn't seen before. In all my staring at that picture, and reading the description of what I wanted so badly, I had never paid attention to the dimensions. This small, cheap plastic doll was exactly what I had ordered. It had never crossed my mind that, as the saying goes, "you get what you pay for." I had never wondered why the magnificent set I was picturing—something that would have been more like an American Girl doll and accessories—would cost only thirty dollars.

I learned some lifelong lessons from that experience. You can believe I (nearly always) remember to check the dimensions on my Amazon purchases. And more significantly, I took a giant step in the ongoing process of tempering my expectations of what my money can buy. I have remembered that experience many times since then, when filled with disappointment in something I thought would bring me happiness, only to find it brought me regret —a reminder of what else I could have done with the money.

I'm not the first to learn this lesson. In fact, most people learn early that at least some of the things they think will make them happy leave them disappointed and disillusioned. Many—including many notable Christians—have immortalized this wisdom in books, poems, songs, and sermons. "All that glitters is not gold," wrote Shakespeare, capturing a bit of ancient philosophy. And people have been proving these words ever since. "Money never made a man happy yet, nor will it. There is nothing in its nature to produce happiness. The more a man has, the more he wants. Instead of its filling a vacuum, it makes one," Benjamin Franklin said. "Can't buy me love," said the Beatles. "You can't buy happiness," said nearly everyone else.

"Chasing after this world makes me tired. Praising my own name leaves me dry," sing the Newsboys in their song "Live with Abandon." And U2 sings, "I still haven't found what I'm looking for." We can all relate to these musicians' feelings. Like them, we have run after paper promises. Like them, we know disappointment and disillusionment. We know the awful emptiness of desires stoked by temporary fulfillment. We know that everything in the catalog is cheaper and smaller than it looks.

The Bible also has a lot to say on this subject, and through his prophets God often corrected his people when they chased illusions. Through Scripture he calls us to a different way of living—one that both makes us more unsatisfied and sets us on a path toward true satisfaction but which, ironically, is not built around our own satisfaction at all.

Yet for some reason, with all this collective clarity at our disposal, we still sometimes chase satisfaction in this world and its party favors. And it does leave us tired and dry. Then, when we finally get wise to the failure of this world to satisfy, we turn our desire for satisfaction on God—and if we're honest, that strategy does not deliver what we hope for.

Feeling satisfied can so easily lead to feeling self-sufficient, believing our hope is in the things we own, the people we love, or our own selves. When we feel unsatisfied, we are more likely to remember we don't have all the answers we need and therefore must lift our eyes to our wise and loving Creator. Embracing unsatisfaction as a permanent condition can help us maintain more consistent focus on him.

EXERCISES

- Chances are, something in your life is pulling your focus away from God and what he wants for you. Chances are, something is tempting you with promises of satisfaction and ultimate happiness. Eventually it will let you down. What is it? What do you need to let go of? Ask for God's help to see through the façade, embrace unsatisfaction, and stop pursuing distractions.

- One way to discover what is taking your focus is to notice what you tend to worry about. What, or whom, are you afraid of losing or giving up? What consumes most of your emotional energy? "Turn your eyes upon Jesus," the old song says, "and the things of earth will grow strangely dim in the light of his glorious grace." Spend some time in worship and offer to God those things that consume your focus. Acknowledge that he owns everything, and affirm your faith and trust in him. You may be blessed with a new sense of focus on what you cannot lose.

- Think back to times when you have been disappointed in something (or someone) you thought would bring you satisfaction, happiness, or peace. Thank God for each of those experiences and the way each pointed you toward him. Thank him that he has not allowed you to become satisfied with lesser things.

Enjoy a
Meaningful Life

❧

One way to actively anticipate our coming
satisfaction is to live a life full of purpose and
meaning while we're unsatisfied. And this
means living for something bigger than ourselves. Even knowing life will not completely
satisfy us, we still have much to live for.

A realistic look at life in an inherently flawed
world is sobering, but its shortcomings aren't
the whole truth about this life; there is a lot of
good news as well. This is a place where love is
on exhibit every day, where science astounds as
it takes us deeper into the mind of our Creator,
where children with stubby crayons hold the
breathtaking power to blithely beautify any ordinary place. This is a place where every single
human being makes an indelible mark simply by
drawing breath on day one.

Abandoning the futile quest for satisfaction—or
the charade that claims we have found it when we
haven't—doesn't mean we have to settle for a miserable life or a pointless one. A life that falls a little

short in gratification can still be full of purpose. In fact, turning away from a focus on filling ourselves can help us clearly see various ways our lives have meaning. This chapter will discuss five of those ways. But first, let's acknowledge the importance of meaning. Not everyone recognizes life as meaningful. But embracing a philosophy that rejects meaning is one of life's reliable recipes for misery.

For many people who lack a sense of meaning, the goal of life becomes the pursuit of happiness. But ironically, happiness by itself can be surprisingly unhealthy. One research study found that people who lack a sense of meaning in their lives can become physically sick as a result, even if these people feel happy. And it gets worse. The scientists conducting the study concluded that happiness without meaning is actually harmful to us.

The study focused on two kinds of happiness: "hedonic well-being" (happiness based in merely experiencing pleasure and avoiding pain) and "eudaimonic well-being" (enjoyment of a meaningful life, built around something bigger than oneself). They tested the impact of both types of happiness on people's physical health and discovered that while eudaimonia, or meaningful life, is good for us, hedonic happiness by itself signals to our bodies that something is wrong. It triggers an inflammatory response in the body, engaging a process designed to protect us from the kinds of injuries and infections that come when people are experiencing chronic adversity. It's the same physical response our bodies might initiate if we were, say, living in a refugee camp. So the pursuit of happiness for its own sake takes its toll on us in the same way that living a difficult life hurts us. Perhaps our bodies just don't believe this kind of happiness is the real thing. "Empty positive emotions are about as good for you for as adversity," said one of the researchers, Barbara Fredrickson.

So if you're looking for a good life, look for meaning. Happiness by itself won't do it. This research simply confirms what many of us already know. We are hard-wired to live meaningful lives. Even if we know how to make ourselves feel good, we don't thrive without a sense of purpose.

Some people who do believe life is meaningful still struggle to see the meaning in their own life. It's hard for them to see how they matter, or maybe acknowledging that their life does matter feels like an act of self-absorption or conceit. But recognized or not, everyone's life does have meaning. And when we stop living for satisfaction, we can discover that meaning in new places. Ultimately, meaning comes from the fact that we are created and loved by God, and we connect with that sense of meaning through living in relationship with him. But knowledge of God and relationship with him are not the only places we can find meaning.

We are made in God's image, and we can't help but show, through our everyday lives, that we matter. What we make of those opportunities is up to us. Consider the following five ways we can find meaning in our lives, even while waiting for the full satisfaction that will come in the next life: knowing our lives have impact, leaving a legacy, participating in creation, seeing change happen, and bearing witness to redemption.

MEANING IN IMPACT

When we are not seeking our own satisfaction, we can focus more on what we give to this world rather than what we get from it. We can find meaning in seeing our fingerprints on the world while we're still in it. The way we live is tremendously important because our actions have influence. This is true for everyone regardless of how skeptical you may be about your own value and influence.

When I work with new coaching clients, we take some time to notice their impact on the world and other people, especially when they're at their best, to help them develop a specific, personal sense of purpose. People have varying degrees of awareness about the kind of impact they make on the others around them, and I'm not surprised when a person doesn't have a good sense for exactly how their lives affect others. It's something I've struggled with myself. But what does surprise me is when people truly believe they don't have any impact on the world around them. Whether from a desire for humility or from a wounded spirit, this sense that we can swim through the stream of life without causing ripples is false.

I understand why the notion of impact can be intimidating. For some, it sounds too much like pride, assumes too much capability or self-importance. For others, it requires taking frightening responsibility for the power they have to bless or curse other people. And for some, denying impact means refusing to face the consequences of their own actions. After all, our good deeds aren't the only ones that influence others. Sometimes we hurt others even when our intentions are good. And when we choose to live only for our own comfort or pleasure, or when we behave self-destructively, we cause damage. Trying to convince ourselves otherwise is an attempt to satisfy ourselves while denying the consequences of our actions. But there is no such thing as a victimless crime. The impact of our actions, good or bad, may be indirect, and it may not be obvious until the next generation. But it always happens.

It really is inescapable: everyone has impact. It can be positive or negative or a mix of both, but as beings made in God's image and made for (and in) relationship from the moment we are born, we cannot go through life without affecting others with our behaviors, words, and attitudes. We have the opportunity to do what we can to produce the kind of world we want to live in, for the common good. This is a blessing to be cherished and part of the awesome God-given power of being human. It's not conceited to believe this, and it is irresponsible to walk around influencing other people with no intention or awareness of what we're doing.

Part of living well is taking ownership of our impact. We need to understand how we affect other people, when we're at our best and at our worst. We all shape the world we live in—either by exerting oppositional influence or by going with the flow. Once we recognize specifically what kind of impact we have, we can embrace it and make it an intentional and inspirational part of our lives. We can make it part of our purpose and sense of meaning in this world. We can make choices that put us in a good position to do for others what we do best—protect them, lead them, accept them, offer them something beautiful. We can hand our best efforts to God as "a living sacrifice, holy and pleasing to God" (Romans 12:1). And in God's hands, our impact becomes much more.

MEANING IN LEGACY

Likewise, we can find meaning in knowing that our impact on the world does not stop when our lives end. Again, this is true of everyone—even those whose names will be forgotten in a few generations. Regardless of how life has met our own longings, our actions matter to younger generations and beyond them, extending to those we will never meet.

In case you haven't already picked up on this, I grew up in a Christian family, where faith was integrated into our everyday lives the same way breathing was. I didn't always appreciate the family devotions or the outdated music on the Christian radio station that played in our home, but I definitely benefitted from the way a relationship with God was matter-of-factly woven into our lives. Christian faith was no hypocritical show for the neighbors.

This part of my family's culture was a reflection of who my parents were. And who they were was a reflection not only of their personal faith but also of the faith of their fathers and mothers. I am blessed to be a descendent of generations of faithful people, most of whom I never knew—I don't even know their names. Yet their choices had a massive, if indirect, impact on me.

Because we can recognize some of the legacy left to us, we know we have the opportunity to bless or curse those who follow us (and most likely we will do both). This is a tremendous perk of human existence. We can pass on our faith, the wisdom we've gained, our genius methods for folding socks and keeping pests out of the garden. And much of what we pass along is entirely unintentional on our part.

I've long been sort of fascinated by the mystery behind Exodus 34:6-7, when God called himself "the compassionate and gracious God, slow to anger, abounding in love and faithfulness, maintaining love to thousands, and forgiving wickedness, rebellion and sin. Yet he does not leave the guilty unpunished; he punishes the children and their children for the sin of the parents to the third and fourth generation." It's not hard to understand the general idea here: our choices reverberate through generations. Our sins have consequences, and those consequences affect others—especially the others who live with us and under our care. We've all seen (and we all live with) the reality of this.

But something here is hard to understand: What exactly does God mean by "punishes the children and their children for the sin of the parents"? Just a glance at this verse in a variety of translations makes it obvious that the concept is not entirely straightforward or clearly understood by translators. For example, the King James Version speaks of "visiting the iniquity of the fathers upon the children." The New American Standard and New Revised Standard versions say something very similar. The New Living Translation says, "I lay the sins of the parents upon their children and grandchildren; the entire family is affected." The New English Translation describes it as "punishing the transgression of fathers by dealing with children and children's children."

A look at the original language reveals at least twenty-five different ways this terminology can be translated into English, including everything from "to pay attention to" to "to be called to account" and "to appoint, assign, deposit." The suggestion is that something intentional is happening—not just an unfolding of natural consequences but an active divine response to rebellion.

So what has God promised to do here? Is this a visitation of punishment for sins committed by those who came before? Or a fancy way of saying that the sins prevalent in the environment we're raised in stick to us and tend to be repeated? Or is there something more here—an actual repetition of the sins themselves? Because the wording seems to suggest that those sins come back to us with a new generation.

A few years ago, reading about a breakthrough scientific study changed the way I read this verse. I learned that scientists have discovered we can change our DNA through our lifestyle choices and our responses to what we experience. It turns out that our habits—exercise, diet, self-care, emotional expression—change our genetic makeup (and determine how our DNA unfolds in our lifetime) and legacy (determining what our children will have to work with). As a result, the DNA we are born with is not necessarily the DNA we will pass on to our descendants.

Perhaps this scientific discovery unravels part of the mystery in Exodus 34:6-7. Yes, our ancestors' actual sins do come back to us because their choices and experiences reshaped their genetic material. They passed on to us not only physical characteristics and family tendencies; they passed on their choices and their responses to the circumstances they found themselves in. No wonder cases of lifestyle-based disease and mental illness are rising among us; no wonder problems like alcoholism and other addictions run in families. We are all living with the proclivities, habits, behaviors, traumas, and joys of those who came before us. And with each generation, the weight of that legacy grows.

Yet we are not mere products of DNA or outcomes of other people's decisions. We are flush with choices big and small. We are dizzy with the power (although often unrecognized) of self-determination. In some ways our lives are strings of choices—some very, very hard, but viable nonetheless. Even if we do not have the power to change our circumstances, our response is in our own hands.

This means we have a grave responsibility to those who will come after us—not only our children, but those we will never meet. Our choices matter not only to us, not only to those we raise, but to everyone who will inherit the genetic material we steward. So, even though our lives are not fully satisfying, they are tremendously valuable. And the more we consider how our lives will shape others, rather than pursue our own satisfaction, the more we will bless the countless people who will live in the wake of our choices.

Sins and the consequences of other people's sins are not the only things we pass on. Things like faithfulness, healing, hard work, physical and mental health, good habits, and generosity reshape us as well. By doing the work of living well, we can change our genetic makeup for the better. And in doing so, we change the impact we have on the world. If our choices reshape our world now, imagine the impact they will have over generations. The choices we make are never just about us.

It can be easy to lose sight of this in a world dripping with celebrity worship, where our significance is often defined by our connections to people who have been on TV—or at least on YouTube. But regardless of the size of your friend list, life in this world really is different because you are in it, and it will be irretrievably changed when you leave it. Your life may not be as deeply satisfying as you want it to be, but it shapes the world others will inhabit. How's that for a meaningful life?

MEANING IN CREATION

Yet ours aren't the only fingerprints we can find all over this world. The marks of God's presence are impossible to miss, ingrained in every atom, even if we overlook them every day. He went way beyond leaving fingerprints—he signed everything.

Psalm 19:1-4 reminds us of just one way God's creative work is made apparent:

> The heavens declare the glory of God;
>> the skies proclaim the work of his hands.
> Day after day they pour forth speech;
>> night after night they reveal knowledge.
> They have no speech, they use no words;
>> no sound is heard from them.
> Yet their voice goes out into all the earth,
>> their words to the ends of the world.

Simply watching the sky is enough to remind us that God's creative power dwarfs our own. To stand in awe of his beautiful, complex work is to find one source of meaning. To care for what he has made is even better.

Yet our participation in creation doesn't stop there. One of God's most generous expressions of creativity was to give us a bit of the same power. We are creative, artistic, practical, and visionary builders with an eye for beauty and function. We are not simply consumers and destroyers. We have been given the capacity to not only appreciate creation but actually create.

I realize some people believe they're not creative; maybe you're one of those people. When people claim they aren't creative, I think what they mean is that they're not fine artists, inventors, or prolific generators of ingenious ideas. Culturally, we tend to think of creativity as a trait belonging to people who are especially gifted in these areas. We forget that absolutely everyone has creative abilities.

We all have ideas, we all know how to put two things together to make something else, and we all know how to use a crayon (or at least we used to). We can find pleasure and meaning in creative work or build something beautiful, sound, or simply functional.

Participating in creation may seem like a small thing, but it's not. To borrow a phrase from Fanny Crosby, it's a foretaste of glory. Everything we create in this world draws its medium and inspiration from what God has made, and ultimately it points back to his genius. Though our creations are temporary, they can point to the permanent. And when we care for our fellow human beings, the pinnacle of God's creation and the ultimate bearers of God's fingerprint, we invest in the eternal.

MEANING IN CHANGE

I've never been a Baptist, but I do love a good baptism. Christenings are heartwarming and unifying, but there's something I relish about hearing people describe their journey and their commitment to Christ, then watching them willingly "take the plunge" before witnesses. In fact, I'll admit I need to see this on a regular basis.

My favorite kind of baptism is the kind where multiple people are baptized in one service, people in different stages of life who have been on dramatically different roads. I saw my children baptized in this kind of service. I love hearing the gospel described by children and by adults, by people who have walked the narrow road and by people who have wandered the wide path and barely lived to tell about it, by people who have just started down the path, armed with an understanding of the gospel that is simpler than it will be in forty years.

I've been in the church my whole life. I got my bachelor's degree from a Christian college. I have spent more than twenty years working in Christian publishing, and most of my writing is aimed at people in the church. Most of my coaching clients call themselves Christians, and the majority of my friends do too. I have everyday interactions with people who believe all kinds of things, including people who are seeking spiritual answers. But I rarely get deeply involved in the life of a person who is undergoing dramatic spiritual transformation. I'll confess it's easy for me to get lost in my own story and forget God still does this kind of work in people. Most of the stories I hear are about refinement— the slower changes God's Spirit works in us over time.

That's why other people's baptisms are very good for my faith. They provide evidence of God's active presence in people and our need for radical change. They remind me of the joy I can access but so often take for granted. They cause me to think about where I would be on my own. They are vulnerable celebrations of utterly undeserved grace.

That grace is our richest source of meaning in life. And regardless of the fact that we cannot see grace clearly or completely in this life, anyone who has come in relationship with Jesus has been, and continues to be, transformed by it. Because of grace, we know circumstances can change. We know people can too! No one is truly stuck or beyond hope. We don't always get what we really deserve, and sometimes we get more than we wished for. Prayers are answered and dreams come true. Habits are broken, relationships are restored. People learn to live with loss and broken hearts start beating smoothly again. The spiritually blind gain sight, and the lost are found.

It's easy to grow weary in this world of wreckage, picking our way through the broken glass of wishes and dreams, flinching at the sound of bursting bubbles. And when we acknowledge we won't find complete satisfaction in this context, discouragement can convince us we are stuck. When we give up the pursuit of total satisfaction, it might be tempting to believe we must give up a life of meaning and purpose. But God sings over us, composing an irrepressible song of delight and hope and invitation to long for what is better. He does not abandon us to what we are, and as we keep our eyes on this everlasting hope of transformation, we can find meaning in both its realization and its potential.

MEANING IN REDEMPTION

Speaking of transformation, it's my favorite kind of redemption. But redemption wears other faces too, and it may be our greatest source for meaning in this life.

As I mentioned earlier, the things that make this world unsatisfying aren't the only things that are true about this life. And the things that make it painful, tragic, and hard to bear aren't the end of the story. This world is in the hands of a God who never walks away, a God who is never overwhelmed, who never fails to see the essence, who never loses sight of the true story. This doesn't mean everything in this world is good. It doesn't justify trite sentiments or sappy formulas for convincing ourselves everything is all right. It doesn't give us a reason to dismiss pain or pretend nothing is broken. It simply means nothing is worthless and no one is hopeless. And it means that when life goes blank, God raises his brush before a prime canvas for some of his most spectacular work—redemption.

My parents would tell you I've always loved fine things, and when I was growing up, I relished an opportunity to pull out the fancy dishes. Now, my family didn't have a set of china or anything like that. But we did have some pretty glasses and serving dishes that made a holiday dinner more festive. And we had a few pieces of silver that I enjoyed polishing. Rubbing the polish on the tarnished surface was like doing a magic trick! Suddenly the dark and smudgy surface would give way to gleam as the true nature of the precious metal shone through. It was very satisfying work.

Polishing silver is an imperfect analogy for redemption. In redemption the value in what is tarnished is brought forth. No matter how much smudge is on the surface, redemption reveals something precious inside. You or your situation might be covered with far more corruption than a little tarnish—you might be rusted or gutted, your circumstances might be full of rot. But God always sees the value in any person and in any situation, and he calls it forth. Sometimes he sands off the rust and makes old things new; sometimes he simply reframes the ugliness and shows us something surprisingly beautiful or uses the smell of decay to create a sweet perfume.

At its core, redemption is not about doing but about seeing value and honoring it: calling it out, setting it free, saving it, exchanging it, rescuing it, purchasing it. God has the ability to see value, often hidden from us, in literally everyone and everything—even people who hurt us and things we hate. And as we grow closer to his heart, he grants us the gift of sometimes seeing the way he does.

When we believe redemption is possible, and can see it for ourselves, we can welcome suffering for what it produces in us. We are able to stop insisting that our lives be satisfying. We can hold our hearts open toward people we're tempted to believe are beyond hope, and can see God glorified in the midst of hardship and horror. We find meaning in anything and everything, even what we so desperately want to be rid of, knowing by faith that God works in all things, that someday redemption will occupy the full stage in the final act of human history, and that creation will be re-created.

IT'S A MEANINGFUL LIFE

In a world that constantly tries to convince us we can find meaning in making ourselves happy, comfortable, or rich, it takes effort to seek meaning elsewhere. Even most of humanity's religious activities are designed not to help us connect with the divine for divinity's sake, but to make us happy, comfortable, or rich. It's tough to consistently live a life full of meaning unless we're ready to live intentionally.

I don't believe that most people who get drunk every weekend want to live in a world where everyone gets drunk every weekend. I don't believe most people who make use of prostitutes, abuse others, behave like monsters on social media, or abuse drugs want to live in a world where everyone makes those same choices. People who indulge in porn generally don't want other people looking at their family members in the same way. People who cheat on their spouses don't want their spouses to cheat on them. They want the rest of the world to behave in kinder and more responsible ways, and they benefit from others' choices to do so, while often happily convincing themselves that what they do isn't hurting anyone. They are living with a profound lack of intention, helping to create exactly the kind of world they don't want to live in.

We all have that same power—and the same tendency when not guided by a sense of right and wrong that lives outside us and feels more important than our appetites. Once we have decided to live with unsatisfaction, if we want to live our most meaningful lives in that context, we must make choices that honor more than just ourselves. We must select the road that leads to the destination we seek, whether it's bumpy or not, regardless of the fact that it will not lead to true and complete satisfaction in this life.

We can start living intentionally by worshiping God for the sake of worshiping God, opening ourselves to a divine agenda rather than asking God to implement ours. We can focus on the work God is doing in the world and invest ourselves in it, recognizing the incredible gift that our actions and choices matter to others. And because of that, we all have the power to make life on this planet a little better or a little worse. We can purposely invest in our legacy, participate in creation, and grieve destruction. We can tenaciously hold to the possibility of transformation and the reality of redemption, open ourselves to both, and believe in them on behalf of others. Intentional living means doing what we can to produce the kind of world we want to live in. It requires taking ownership of our choices. And after we have stopped trying to make life something it isn't, intentional living can infuse every day with meaning.

Blessings of the Unsatisfied Life:
THE BLESSING OF COMPANY

Unsatisfaction can push us toward relationships with other people. And despite pious claims to the contrary, God wants us to desire and enjoy each other's company. He has not entered our lives to displace the human relationships he calls good.

It's a popular myth among believers: if you're sufficiently close to Jesus, all your relational needs will go away. Many buy into claims like the Oswald Chambers declaration I mentioned earlier in this book: "When once we get intimate with Jesus we are never lonely, we never need sympathy, we can pour out all the time without being pathetic." In other words, if you know Jesus, you don't need anybody else. And if you feel a longing for connection beyond what you have, you must not be intimate with Christ.

Loneliness is not a sin, nor should we feel ashamed to acknowledge our desire for relationships. Loneliness is a kind of pain. And as we know from the way our marvelous systems work, pain is never the real problem. Pain is a symptom, an indication of need. Loneliness is a symptom of two needs: our need to be connected to other people and our need for connection with God.

When we were growing up, my younger sister was my best friend. But my older sister and I didn't get along well. She was three years older than me, and I felt envious of the privileges and attention she got—the fact that she was older and able to do more just never seemed right to me. And I took it out on her. As for why she didn't like me, well, I was her bratty little sister who was always competing with her and picking fights with her. I was probably hard for her to like. We went through times when we fought a lot, and other times we mostly ignored each other.

When she left home and went to college, she didn't go far— her school was in the same city. At that point we weren't sharing space and competing for resources, and we started to get along better. She even let me hang out with her and her cool college friends sometimes.

But it wasn't until I had my first child that my sister started to look like a potential friend. In those early days of motherhood, living in Alaska and far away from all family members, I started reaching out to my sisters, who were both mothers before me, for advice. And in addition to mothering advice, I needed connections to people who had known me for a long time. If you have sisters, you'll probably agree there's no one like a sister to fit that bill.

As we got in touch, I realized my big sister was a really nice person and we actually had a lot in common (to a spooky degree). We began talking on the phone every now and then. I began getting to know her as a friend. When we moved from Alaska to the "lower forty-eight," we started getting together. And our relationship blossomed into a friendship that is one of the greatest blessings in my life today. Now I'm close to both my sisters, and I'm so thankful God used my need for connection and advice to push me toward them and forge a new friendship with one.

The importance of human relationships was affirmed way back in the beginning of human history, when God created Eve (Genesis 2:18-23). "It is not good for the man to be alone," God declared. Adam had unbroken fellowship with God before sin entered the world, yet God did not expect this relationship to satisfy all Adam's needs. Apparently neither did God consider the creation of one human sufficient to fully express what he wanted to express through creation. He called it "not good," in contrast to his other pronouncements about what he had made. Only after he had created both male and female (Genesis 1:27) did he call his creation "very good" (Genesis 1:31).

Elsewhere in Scripture we see affirmation that we are created to enjoy relationships with each other. Our relational nature is one element of what it means for us to be made in God's image—the Trinity is a relational God. Jesus himself modeled the value of relationships for us in his life on earth.

Like the people we see represented in Scripture, we long for unbroken relationship with God; we were meant for that. We also need relationships with each other, and that desire is a good, God-given one.

God commonly uses this need in our lives. We may never be more in touch with our relational needs than when we feel unsatisfied. We may never be more willing to do the work required to make a relationship healthy, loving, and transformational.

As Gillian Marchenko wrote in her book *Still Life*, discussing her battle with major depressive disorder, "I cannot begin to understand why so many, indeed all of us, struggle on earth. But when I think about the Trinity in perfect community with one another, I can't help but think that our struggles and our pain pull community out of us sinners who otherwise would think we were happy and filled up with Facebook and *Grey's Anatomy* reruns."

If you feel lonely, it can mean something is wrong. It can also mean something is right. It can mean you are in touch with your longing for the kind of world you were actually made for. And it can drive you to seek out relationships you might avoid if you felt fully satisfied, relationships in which God wants to reveal himself to and through you.

EXERCISES

- How is your search for satisfaction creating barriers between you and other people, or keeping you from recognizing your need for relationships? Maybe you numb your emotions with food, shopping, substances, or work, rather than share them with caring people. Perhaps you have a hard time slowing down long enough to have a real conversation. Seek some support from a counselor, coach, or addiction recovery group. As you get in touch with your needs, let that sense of unsatisfaction push you toward healthy relationships without the expectation that they will placate all your desires.

- Make a commitment to do your part to create a culture of authenticity within your sphere. You can start by being honest with yourself, and with God, about your lingering sense of unsatisfaction. As you become more genuine and open, you will inspire others to do the same.

- Create margins in your life to allow room for relationships. Quit something, get up earlier, put down your phone, block out "Holy Spirit time" on your calendar. Then reach out to other unsatisfied people for some genuine connection.

Look for
Fulfillment

❧

If you think embracing unsatisfaction means spending your days mired in unappeased longing, think again. There's no reason we should be aimless, and there's no reason we can't pursue fulfillment. Fulfillment is different from the kind of satisfaction our souls long for. Fulfillment means finding a match between our needs and desires and what will gratify them. Most of the time it's a temporary condition, and with maturity and growth we come to see that fulfillment doesn't call for permanence or perfection—it's like eating a meal when we're hungry, knowing we will be hungry again. Ultimate satisfaction, on the other hand, calls for our hunger to be permanently neutralized, satiated once and for all. When we don't confuse it with satisfaction, fulfillment can be a good guiding goal in our lives.

Sometimes people feel nervous about the idea of seeking fulfillment. It sounds self-indulgent, self-important, maybe even hedonistic. But this need not be true. We all have desires that might lead us to gratify ourselves at the expense of others or that might cause us to destroy ourselves, and it's not a good idea to follow these impulses. But those aren't the only desires we possess. As Jen Pollock Michel writes in her excellent book *Teach Us to Want*, "Although easily corrupted, desire is good, right and necessary. It is a force of movement in our lives, a means of transportation. It can be the very thing that motivates us to change and that carries us to God. Growing into maturity doesn't mean abandoning our desires, but growing in our discernment of them."

Sometimes it seems a great many people believe God wants us to be miserable—perhaps while pretending to be happy, maybe while grimly watching the world go by. After all, "Jesus said to his disciples, 'Whoever wants to be my disciple must deny themselves and take up their cross and follow me'" (Matthew 16:24). Self-denial means we never get what we want, right? Wrong! Humbly submitting your will to God's, offering everything you are and everything you have to his service, even living with a willingness to die for the sake of faithfulness to him, does not mean rejecting the gifts he gives us and places within us. In fact, sacrificing and submitting to him can be fulfilling in themselves, and they can fit with the desires he's given us.

Sometimes I work with coaching clients who are thinking of changing jobs and feel guilty for thinking of leaving their current employers. Their desire to move on feels like disloyalty and ingratitude to the organizations they work for. It also can feel like rejection of something God has provided for them. For some people, it takes a lot of work to overcome the feeling that making a change is somehow wrong—even if they are desperately unhappy or seriously disengaged from their work and perhaps even finding themselves opposing their employers' goals. I worked with one woman—I'll call her Tonya—who was miserable every day. She felt trapped in her job, and she wasn't in full agreement with the stated mission and values of the faith-based organization she worked for. She found herself daydreaming about not only a different job but an entirely different career. I had no doubt that if her employer knew her low level of engagement, they would agree it was time to move on. In fact, it's possible her work there was counterproductive because her heart wasn't in it. Yet she had to wrestle with the sense that it was somehow wrong to want something different for herself—and that her employer would be angry at the thought of her disloyalty.

Tonya did make a change. She came to a place of recognition that staying in her job was hurting her and possibly hurting others. She left her job and was stunned to discover the freedom and joy in letting go of this ill-fitting position. And someone else had the opportunity to move into a new and fulfilling role.

Contrary to popular belief, it is not necessarily selfish to desire a change in circumstances. Are we loving God and loving other people in those changes? Are we honoring God's commands? These are illuminating questions we must ask ourselves. If the change you desire means divorcing your spouse so you can marry a younger model—yes, that is a selfish option. It doesn't mean the core desire behind that impulse (for a more harmonious marriage relationship, for example) is bad, but it certainly means the desire must be examined and redirected. If your desires are leading you to look for a new job that might be a better fit for you, this probably is not wrong, assuming you are caring for the people you need to care for and living as God would have you live. In fact, it may be a wonderful move that benefits many people as you open your spot for someone who's dreaming of your current job and you take on a new role where you will have great results because you're engaged and well-suited to the work.

Sometimes we think what we want doesn't matter. But God shapes our desires and uses our desires to shape us. Stating what we want can be a powerful expression of our beliefs, our values, our gifts, and our sense of purpose. That doesn't mean we will always get what we want. It doesn't give us the right to insist on everything we want. But it can form the foundation of stepping into roles God has designed us for.

Remember, we were created for a better world, in which our desires would always lead us to good things. While we, along with our desires and their objects, have been corrupted by sin, our desires are still gifts that can lead us to good things. Think of the desires that lead us into friendships, motivate us to produce children and to love them, encourage us to care for ourselves, haunt us into creating something beautiful, drive us to explore, and beckon us toward God and obedience. We were made with desires that were made to be fulfilled. It's wise to pay attention to our desires (with a healthy skepticism, realizing we can easily rationalize something that is wrong), recognizing that God uses our desires to lead us.

When I was somewhere around twelve years old, my mom bought a pattern and decided to make some shirts for my sisters and me. She was (and is) a great seamstress, and she would occasionally make something special for us. I was ecstatic over this particular project because I got to pick out my own fabric and the pattern was for what we referred to then as a "big shirt," the height of fashion for teenage girls in the mid-1980s. I chose a red-and-white striped fabric, and when my mom was finished making the shirt, I was absolutely thrilled with it.

To put this story in context, I need to tell you that for most of my growing years, I wore hand-me-downs almost exclusively. Rarely, this meant simply wearing something my older sister had worn. More often, it meant wearing something my older sister had worn after receiving it in a bag of clothes donated by a family in the church with multiple daughters, who had all worn it before they outgrew it and gave it to the pastor's daughters. As you might imagine, this meant my clothes were rarely stylish.

When Mom presented me with this oversize red-and-white-striped shirt, I was so happy. I loved it, and I couldn't wait to wear it. But suddenly I felt troubled by my own delight. This unaccustomed feeling felt like sinful self-indulgence. I remember asking Mom, "Is it okay to have something this nice?" I was sincerely concerned that it was wrong for a Christian to have something truly nice and stylish. And my mom wisely assured me that while nothing should interfere with our worship and reverence for God, it was fine to have a stylish shirt.

Even though we can't achieve perfect satisfaction in this life, and we won't always get it right, we can pursue a good life. We can pursue achievement of our best self—fully developing the potential God has placed in us. We can match our good desires with the best expressions of what we long for. And one way to pursue fulfillment is through paying attention to our alignment.

POINTS OF ALIGNMENT

Alignment, applied to an individual, occurs when various parts of that person's life line up appropriately, all pointing in the same direction and not crossing or interfering with each other. Alignment is an important piece of fulfillment—and of living a healthy life. When we're out of alignment, we find ourselves in a conflict of sorts that demands resolution and, if unresolved, keeps us from feeling fulfilled and takes its toll on our well-being. That conflict may be with our environment (as with a teetotaler in a bar on a Saturday night) or it may be within ourselves (like when a vegetarian develops a craving for meat). As one psychologist put it, "Recognizing that we are acting in opposition to our values creates an internal experience of being divided. This, in turn, leads to varying degrees of discomfort and psychological conflict. Ongoing conflict can result in the development of physical symptoms, such as anxiety, insomnia or overeating." People whose lives are well aligned enjoy harmony among their sense of purpose, stated values, and spiritual beliefs. They are able to express their sense of purpose and their personal values in their everyday decisions. Anyone who can't do this will be profoundly uncomfortable with his or her circumstances, often without realizing why.

For most of us, the true consequences of non-alignment are not public, or even external, but internal. That conflict within us does its damage at our core. Eventually, the destruction spills over and shows itself in our relationships and our behavior. Clinical psychologist Dr. Edward Dreyfus maintains, "It is my belief that many of the symptoms of psychological stress with which people struggle and for which they seek psychotherapy are exacerbated, if not caused by, living lives without integrity. . . . I contend that it is not possible to feel a sense of personal wholeness and feeling of internal integration while living in ways that undermine one's integrity."

As followers of Christ, bringing our lives into alignment means starting with our general calling as Christians. We are made in God's image and called to reflect his qualities and to do what God asks of us. If a person's life is out of step with this calling, everything else will be pointing in the wrong direction or will not have the support it needs when tested. Fulfillment will come only after realignment.

Human beings are made for alignment, and when we try to maintain more than one version of ourselves, eventually the effort will destroy us. It keeps us from being known and loved for who we are, it makes us into hypocrites, and it leaves us without a strong sense of our strengths, weaknesses, and limitations. It also leaves us unfulfilled.

BUILDING ON PURPOSE

Another important component of fulfillment is building a life that reflects our unique sense of purpose, in addition to our general calling as children of God. This is related to the sense of meaning discussed in chapter five, but it is more specific. Every life has meaning; in order for us to feel fulfilled, we must also feel we as individuals are living for some kind of specific purpose.

Here's one way I describe my unique sense of purpose: to be a quietly blazing fire that heats the room with beauty, truth, and wisdom. This statement reflects my personality, the impact I tend to have on other people, and some of the things that are most important to me. If I try, I can find people who have a sense of purpose very similar to mine. And, in fact, when I work with coaching clients to create their own purpose statements, occasionally I hear one that overlaps a little with mine. But I'll bet no one else in the world would describe their purpose in exactly the way I've done so. And some people have a dramatically different idea of what they're here for. This is by God's design—we are very different people. After all, I'm not cut out to be a wildfire, dramatically changing the landscape in an instant. And those who are would never be content to blaze quietly, merely heating the room and reflecting on the people there. At the same time, I am not content to be in a room without changing the temperature in some way. People come in spectacular variety. God is not a one-dimensional being whose image can be captured in a single human personality. God can't even be accurately represented by the entire human race. God makes us different, and our unique qualities matter! They are part of our purpose.

Chances are, you're living with some kind of purpose, even if you haven't stated what it is. If you don't live with your own sense of purpose, someone else will likely to define your purpose for you—and it will probably mean recruiting you to help fulfill the purpose

God gave them (or a purpose they have given themselves). Part of seeking fulfillment is to be intentional about your impact and consider how best to be the person God has made you to be. Maybe your purpose, up to this point, has been to find true satisfaction in life. Maybe that purpose can now become something new.

While a sense of purpose will not ultimately satisfy all your longings, it is a great starting point for living a fulfilling life—a life that reflects a match between the way God has made you and how you use what God has given you.

RESPECT PERSONAL VALUES

Another important element in pursuing fulfillment is recognizing and living in line with our personal values—the things that are most important to us. Our values help make us who we are, and they act as powerful motivators for us. Ignoring them can lead us into circumstances, relationships, or habits that keep us from flourishing and having the influence God wants us to have. Recognizing and finding ways to respect these values can help us remain true to our God-shaped intentions on even our worst days.

Values come in different brands. We all have moral values that define right and wrong for us. These values are determined by our religious beliefs, our family of origin, maybe the culture we live in (whether we are in agreement or opposition). We also have personal values that are not about right and wrong; they're about what is most important to us as individuals. We probably have some of these values in common with others around us, but we also each have values that differ, and some of our values may even conflict with the values of people we know and love. This kind of conflict can create tension, misunderstanding, and competing goals. But these values aren't about moral right and wrong.

For example, excellence is one of my strong values. And back when I was in high school and working at Burger King, I worked alongside some people who shared my value of excellence . . . and some who definitely did not. I'm not sure what these teenage boys valued most, but let's be generous and say it was something like (ahem) efficiency. Well, we had a clash of values that created some minor conflict. I say "minor" because there wasn't much back and forth happening. It was mostly a matter of me firmly chastising some of my fellow employees and passing along the lesson that putting dirty plastic trays in a sink full of dirty water is unlikely to result in clean plastic trays (you're welcome, customers). And I think my arguments were pretty compelling (and they got results). But they had a point they could have made as well: we also needed to be efficient and quick in our work. After all, it was supposed to be fast food. So we couldn't spend all our time cleaning the trays. While it's important to adhere to high standards of cleanliness in food service, regardless of your personal values, it's not wrong to value efficiency or to value excellence. In fact, valuing excellence while losing sight of efficiency would have created its own disasters. There's no real moral question here; it's a matter of personal values and learning how to honor both, probably with some compromise involved.

While it's critical for us to honor our moral values if our lives are going to be fulfilling and bring honor to God, in many ways they're also easier to honor than our personal values. Moral values often feel like "shoulds," and they are likely reinforced by many of the people we hang around. They often produce a sense of guilt when they're crossed. So most people don't need to be encouraged to identify them and affirm that they're important—even if we all fail to live up to our own moral standards at times. Personal values are different. Many of us don't have a good understanding of our values, even though they drive much of our behavior and our feelings about life circumstances. It can be harder for us to assert these nonmoral values.

When I work with clients, in addition to describing their life purpose, we also identify personal values, considering what's most important to them. Then we look at how they can honor those personal values in their everyday lives. Identifying values can help us understand why we feel fulfilled or frustrated in our work, relationships, churches, and circumstances. Often we feel a sense of dissatisfaction, frustration or even anger, but we don't understand why. Sometimes we dismiss our frustration or anger as simple whining or inappropriate complaining. But sometimes they are much more significant than that. Often they're indicators that we're in circumstances where our personal values are being violated. We may even be the ones violating them.

When we're oblivious to our personal values, we don't understand what drives some of our behavior. We make choices based on our values, whether we recognize them or not. Sometimes we feel paralyzed by indecision because we're facing a conflict between two or more of our values, and, if we don't know what our values are, we don't have the tools we need to choose between them. Coming to understand our values puts us in the position to live intentionally, to make choices for ourselves, and to express what matters most to us. Understanding our values helps us better understand where other people are coming from too, and it empowers us to make choices to honor their values as well as ours. In short, it helps us love others better and form relationships that can last and be mutually life-giving rather than feeding one person while the other person's spirit dries up. And knowing what we value is a great way to equip ourselves for a life that is, while not ultimately satisfying to our souls, fulfilling.

LIFE-GIVING RELATIONSHIPS

One of the most critical foundations of a fulfilling life is our relationships. Especially considering our spouses or significant others, our best friends, and other people we're close to, who strongly influence the way we live.

I'm a big fan of *The Lord of the Rings* books. These great stories teach us many lessons, one of which is the importance of the company we keep. In the trilogy, Frodo Baggins is charged with destroying the dominant "ring of power" so it cannot be used for its evil intended purpose: ruling over—and destroying—all creatures in Middle Earth. Although Frodo is the one destined to complete this task, he cannot do it alone. The other beings in the "fellowship of the ring" play critical roles in helping Frodo. They all make sacrifices and exercise incredible bravery, most of which Frodo never witnesses, to ensure he can complete his task. And his most faithful friend, Samwise Gamgee, literally carries Frodo at the end of his journey, when exhaustion and spiritual oppression overwhelm him, and enables him to complete the job. Some (myself included) might argue Sam is the real hero of the story.

As in fiction, our real-life relationships are powerful. We are quick to point this out to our children and other young people we influence, but we sometimes forget it's true for adults too. We are always capable of growth and change, and we are shaped by our associates over the course of our lives.

Do your beliefs, sense of meaning and purpose, and values line up with those of the people closest to you? Do you at least have some significant overlap? If so, you'll all be more fulfilled and effective than you could be on your own. But if not, where will those relationships take you over the long term? What needs to change so you can all honor what is most important to you? How can you build on the things you do hold in common? These can be scary questions to ask about relationships, but there's a part of you (perhaps a painful part) that is already asking them, and they merit open consideration.

Other relationships matter too. The people we interact with on a regular basis will either reinforce or contradict the things that are most important to us. They will either honor or dishonor our values—and they can honor our values even if they don't agree with us. They will help us move closer to God and to a life that honors him (even if they don't follow Christ), or they will point us in another direction. It's a good idea to consider whether our relationships are fortifying us or undermining our intentions for the way we want to live. When we experience conflict or mismatch in a relationship, that relationship doesn't necessarily need to end. Simply acknowledging the tension may lead to greater understanding, help us move closer to one another, or make us decide to enforce important boundaries.

The importance of our relationships extends to the virtual world as well. The media we choose to engage have a privileged role in our lives as we allow them—most of whom are strangers to us—to speak into our lives and our perspective.

When we're seeking to live well, it's important that we don't confuse satisfaction with fulfillment. No relationship can possibly satisfy all our needs, desires, and ideals; with the exception of Christ, no person can live up to that kind of expectation. But our relationships can be fulfilling, meeting some of our wants and needs in wonderful ways that reflect the image of God.

WORK

Like many of you, I've held a variety of jobs in my day. And I've worked for a wide variety of organizations. I already mentioned my high school job at Burger King, where I took orders, ran the cash register, and worked the drive-thru. Because this was my first "real" job (besides babysitting and cleaning houses), I learned a lot in that role—important lessons and principles that have applied to every job I've held since. In fact, I've learned important lessons and skills at every single one of the jobs I've held. However, some of these jobs were a terrible fit for me. I'm thinking, in particular, of my jobs as a data entry technician (where my creative mind nearly wasted away), a server in a restaurant (where my hyperfocused and perfectionistic tendencies made me a disaster), and a telemarketer (where I loathed myself for what I was doing to people). If there's a list of rankings out there showing the personalities most and least likely to enjoy calling people and trying to sell them something over the phone, I'm pretty sure my personality (maybe even my name) would be at the bottom of that list. The only thing I had going for me was that I was exceptionally skilled at reading the script without stumbling over my words. I survived it for a summer, but no matter how much they paid me, there was never any chance I was going to be fulfilled by sitting in a cubicle and calling strangers, trying to convince them to switch long-distance carriers. And it wasn't only the duties of the job—I couldn't stomach the whole idea.

No matter how intentional and purposeful we are in our private lives, we will never fit neatly with employers whose mission and values conflict with our own. As consumer brands know, we are much more likely to continue our association with organizations if they espouse mission statements and values we admire. And strong companies understand the importance of inspiring this kind of harmony within their organizations as well. This makes perfect sense. As in other relationships, our sense of fulfillment is greater when we're in relationship with organizations that support our sense of purpose and what is most important to us.

For example, consider these mission statements:

- Starbucks' mission is "to inspire and nurture the human spirit—one person, one cup and one neighborhood at a time."

- McDonald's mission is "to be our customers' favorite place and way to eat and drink."

- Purina's mission is "helping pets live longer, happier and healthier lives through proper nutrition and care."

- Shell Oil's mission, in part, is "to continuously deliver shareholder value by manufacturing and supplying oil products and services that satisfy the needs of our customers."

- Google's mission is "to organize the world's information and make it universally accessible and useful."

- Christianity Today, the company I most recently worked for, has this mission: "equipping Christians to renew their minds, serve the church, and create culture to the glory of God."

- My church's mission is "to lead people into a transformational relationship with Jesus Christ and impact our world through his grace."

Personally, I don't think I would find much fulfillment in working for a company whose mission is simply "to deliver shareholder value" or "to be our customers' favorite place." But some people wouldn't have any interest in helping pets live longer or inspiring people with coffee. And many could never be happy at a workplace like my most recent one, which includes "Christians," "the church," and "the glory of God" in the same sentence. When we're considering working, or even volunteering, for an organization, it's worth speculating on what these true guiding principles are and whether they match up with our own.

When we're able to express and honor some of our personal values in our work, without experiencing a lot of conflict between our values and the organization's values, we're much more likely to feel fulfilled by our involvement. We'll also probably be valued by others in the organization. When people inside an organization share a common sense of purpose, the organization's momentum will be moving clearly in one direction, increasing likelihood that the organization can actually pursue and fulfill its mission.

Again, if we look to our work to completely satisfy us, it will always fall short. But fulfillment of some of our dreams and goals is possible, and it is far more likely when we think through what is most important to us and seek an organization that shares some of our interests and goals.

WHY FULFILLMENT MATTERS

So why is fulfillment important? It's important because the way we live our lives matters, and we are most likely to live in keeping with God's purposes for us when we seek a life that is fulfilling. That doesn't mean we'll always be happy, safe, healthy, or settled. But we can find fulfillment in our lives without any of these things.

Many of us go through life mostly reacting to what comes our way. We find ourselves thrown around by life's circumstances and eventually forget the power of our own intention. We forget that while we can't control all our circumstances, we do get to decide how we will respond. While we don't get to make all our dreams come true, we do get to choose what to strive for. And while our lives will not be completely satisfying, we do get to orient our lives around the things that matter most to us.

We weren't put here to build a life that satisfies our every longing and quells our hunger and thirst in an instant. Each of us was put here to know God and to express the image of God in the form it takes in us. Remember that fulfillment is different from true satisfaction. It can bring a sense of satisfaction for a time, or in certain areas of life, but it will not truly quench our thirst, and we'll grow restless again. We will live best if we do not ask too much of fulfillment. We should not expect it to be complete, once and for all. And we should not expect it to bring us ultimate satisfaction.

In fact, fulfillment is always temporary. As life changes, we have to keep reassessing our sense of fulfillment. As we lose sight of God and his plans, we have to make adjustments. As others go astray (friends, organizations, workplaces, leaders we follow), we have to rethink the relationships in our lives. Living with purpose is not the same as living with perfection. Life is not perfect, nor will it satisfy us, but deep fulfillment comes from moving in the right direction, seeing progress, seeing that our lives have purpose and that God can use even our shortcomings and screw-ups.

Blessings of the Unsatisfied Life: THE BLESSING OF GROWTH

Unsatisfaction serves as one of our primary motivators for pursuing personal growth. While we might want to grow because we think we'll be rewarded with money, status, or something else, the truth is we rarely want to submit ourselves to the process of change unless we experience a measure of unsatisfaction with the way we are—or the way our lives are working.

In the 1980s, Japanese business exported a concept originally imported from American business after World War II. Western businesses became enamored with the Japanese concept *kaizen,* which means "change for the better" and which American businesses generally call "continuous improvement." Kaizen is a process of intentionally making changes—big and small—to products and processes so that they're always improving. Over time, the small changes add up to big innovation. Kaizen holds everyone responsible for continuous improvement, from executives to the people who track inventory and keep the books. Along with its results, kaizen is interesting for what it reveals about the human attraction to inertia. When we achieve success, continuously improving on our efforts doesn't come naturally; we have to build processes and discipline ourselves to reject satisfaction.

Satisfied people are often self-satisfied people. If our circumstances and our emotions suggest nothing is broken, we think, "Why fix it?" We're motived to change when something in our environment, our relationships, or our spirit tells us we need to change—not often because we simply see it for ourselves.

A veteran of five back surgeries, I am very familiar with the experience of physical therapy. And I hate it. I hate all the time it takes. The small-muscle work. The exercises, working the parts of you that most want to be left alone. Even the massages you get at physical therapy, generally speaking, don't feel good. But whenever I have done physical therapy, I have jumped in and worked hard, determined to rehabilitate my body and overcome both the pain of injury and the dysfunctions that landed me in the surgeon's office in the first place. Without major injury and the desire to recover from surgery, there's no way I would have spent my time and energy on those exercises. I just wouldn't do physical therapy for fun. My pain and limitations made me unsatisfied with my body the way it was, and I was motivated to put in the work because I wanted my life to be better.

The ultimate form of personal growth is sanctification, the process through which God transforms us, more and more, into the image of Christ. This process requires our cooperation— obedience to God's Word and submission to his will for us. And our cooperation begins with desire. If we do not want to be more holy, we will resist the process of sanctification at every step. On the other hand, if we want to become more like Christ, God will meet us in that desire and revolutionize us from the inside out— often in ways we would not have chosen for ourselves. That desire for Christlike change is a gift from God, but we can choose to foster it, suppress it, or attempt to meet it with lesser forms of growth that are less likely to threaten our very nature. The more unsatisfied we are with what we can make of our own lives, the more open we are to God's radical work in us.

Our sense of unsatisfaction can keep us from believing we are fine just as we are. It can fuel a desire to know God more and continuously welcome his transformation in us.

EXERCISES

- Spiritual disciplines are practices designed to help us grow and to welcome God's work in us. Consider adding a new form of discipline to your life, at least for a time. For ideas, check out a ministry like Renovaré or one of the many books, new and classic, on the subject.

- Read Romans 5:1-6. As pain is part of rehabilitation in physical therapy, God often uses suffering to help us grow. How are you suffering now? Rather than simply ask God to end your suffering, thank him for how he will use your suffering to help you grow and change. Ask him how he wants you to cooperate with his work in and through your pain.

- Nothing helps you take your eyes off your own unsatisfied self—and grow at the same time—like serving others. Through your church or a local ministry, find an opportunity to spend some time helping people in need.

Appreciate the Gift of Pleasure

Pleasure can sound like a dirty word.

But it's not. Pleasure is a gift from God, and kept in its appropriate place in our lives, pleasure is an important element of living well while awaiting full satisfaction.

As with many of God's good gifts, our ideas about pleasure have been corrupted by human sin and idolatry, by misuse and abuse. Often the idea of pleasure is associated with activities that bring regret and remorse, things done in secret and without restraint. It might bring to mind the excesses of ancient Rome, the Dionysian festivals of ancient Greece. For me it evokes memories of seeing Pleasure Island in Disney's movie *Pinocchio* (which really freaked me out as a child), the cursed amusement park where all the bad boys go to drink, smoke, and eventually transform into donkeys. It's reminiscent of Cookie Monster's out-of-control consumption, his life revolving around the only thing that really makes him happy. In your imagination, it might look like Jabba the Hutt of

Star Wars, living off other people's misery, belching in his lair, surrounded by creatures enslaved merely for his amusement. It might evoke tragic and all-too-real visions of the streets of Bangkok or Vegas, frat parties, or the hookup culture on some college campuses and in night clubs (and in stupid comedy movies aimed at young men). They're scenes of unbridled appetite, self-destruction, victimization, and disgust.

Providing contrast are ascetics, who foreswear everything but the one thing they consider essential for life, so they might focus only on that. For early Christians like the desert fathers and mothers, that one thing was intimacy with Christ. Everything else had to go. So they swore off all life's pleasures and withdrew from society to live solitary lives or to form monastic communities in the Middle Eastern desert. Francis of Assisi was a famous ascetic, founder of the Franciscan order and advocate of the virtues of poverty and humility.

Especially when set against a life of hedonism, it's easy to assume a life of poverty and grim repudiation of our desires is the Christian ideal. And one might expect a book about living an unsatisfied life to espouse such a view. After all, Jesus talked about self-denial and told more than one person to give up everything in order to be a true follower (Luke 12:33; 14:33; 18:22). But Jesus never gave a universal command that all his followers get rid of everything or live in poverty or misery. He never told us to reject God's good gifts. Instead, he has taught us to keep pleasure in its proper place, and that's what an intentionally unsatisfied life calls for. Christ clearly does require that people value him more than anything else and that we recognize God is the true owner of everything we might be tempted to believe we possess. He has also created us with appetites meant to lead us to him, and he has placed us in a world full of color, music, and dizzying flavors.

Pleasure is not a dirty word. It's a gift from God himself. God is the inventor of pleasure, and like all creation it was made to

express something about who God is. When we give up our
pursuit of complete satisfaction here and now, we are not required
to reject enjoyment. When we accept the good pleasures of life,
gifts from God's own hand, we not only appreciate life more; we
better understand God and experience a taste of what is to come.
We can enjoy what God has given us without demanding that it
fulfill all our longings. In fact, when we commit to live an unsatisfied life, we strengthen our position in the face of temptation to
worship pleasure and center our lives around its pursuit. We have
no need to renounce our enjoyment of life when we keep it in its
proper place.

ENJOY!

In C. S. Lewis's *Screwtape Letters,* the fictional demon Screwtape
makes an important point of correction to his nephew and protégé
Wormwood. He suggests finesse is required when attempting to
lure a man into ruin through pleasures:

> Never forget that when we are dealing with any pleasure in
> its healthy and satisfying form, we are, in a sense, on the
> Enemy's ground. I know we have won many a soul through
> pleasure. All the same, it is His [God's] invention, not ours.
> He made the pleasures: all our research so far has not enabled
> us to produce one. All we can do is encourage the humans to
> take the pleasures which our Enemy has produced, at times,
> or in ways, or in degrees, which he has forbidden.

Pleasure is not inherently wicked; it's inherently good and frequently misused. It's a gift best handled with care.

We are created with wholesome human desires—for things like
loving relationships with other people, beautiful places, meaningful
work, leaving a legacy—that God gives us and expects us to honor. As
I've mentioned elsewhere in this book, these desires can be corrupted.

But it's not safe to assume God is honored when we deny our desires or try to will them away. He is honored when we accept his gifts and delight in them, remaining within the boundaries of obedience to him and loving care for our neighbors.

God reveals himself to us through our enjoyment of the natural world. He teaches us through relationships with the people around us. He loves us and cares for us both by giving us needs and by providing the things that will fulfill those needs: sleep, food, water, warmth. He has blessed us with senses that can make nearly any experience a five-dimensional celebration. He has given us all an eye for beauty and some of us the skill to capture it and share it with everyone else. He made a world complex enough that all of human history has not been enough to exhaust the pleasure of discovery. Life in this world is full of good things, and God has given us great capacity to enjoy them. We can do so while acknowledging no amount of God's good gifts will substitute for God's presence and his making all things new. We can enjoy the good things in life without demanding that life give us only pleasure or that it give us everything our souls need.

For example, after I travel and speak somewhere I always come home exhausted, sometimes depleted. I know I need to take a day off, so I plan for it—particularly if I have been gone over the weekend. I usually sleep in, start the day slowly, and use the time to catch up on things that have piled up in my absence, as well as relax. This is a necessity for my well-being, but it's also pleasurable. If I decided I enjoyed these days so much I was going to live like that every day, that indulgence would become a problem for me and the people who depend on me. But keeping it in its proper place is not a problem; I can enjoy the pleasures of a day off without demanding a life of leisure.

Belief in the inherent wickedness of pleasure is not the only reason we sometimes feel uncomfortable indulging. We also engage in emotional self-protection and what I call "thrivers guilt." Emotional self-protection is a strategy we use to try to shield ourselves from some of the impact of pain and disappointment. Knowing that life brings both pain and pleasure, we hesitate to enjoy the good things because we know they won't last, and we fear the hard times will hurt more for having enjoyed ourselves.

But walking through life grimly, focusing only on the negative, doesn't provide an effective insurance policy against being hurt by times of darkness or scarcity. In fact, it can make the dark times that much darker and harder to bear because they are not mitigated by the effects of light. It's a mark of maturity, emotional capacity, and courage when a person can embrace life's dual realities of pleasure and pain without allowing one to scare us away from the other.

Thrivers guilt is a similar denial of pleasure, ostensibly for the sake of others. But like self-protection, it is really about our own comfort. We feel awkward enjoying ourselves in light of the knowledge that others are suffering—or even simply that they are not enjoying themselves as much as we are. So we deny ourselves enjoyment in an effort to resolve our internal conflict.

Thrivers guilt is one of the things that can keep caregivers from caring for themselves, gifted people from succeeding beyond the expectations of their communities, free people from living as if they are free. Sometimes this guilt is induced by social pressure; sometime we're just uncomfortable knowing that someone somewhere doesn't have what we have. We know we don't really deserve to be happier or more comfortable than other people, and our awareness that many people are deprived when we're prospering, miserable when we're happy, enslaved when we're free, bored when we're flourishing, can keep us from enjoying or even accepting what we have.

I am not advocating callousness or a way of life that ignores the price others pay for our prosperity or refuses to share with others.

We must live in a way that improves the lives of others, as far as it is within our power. But refusing to enjoy our own good blessings—loving families, physical and mental health, relative safety, adequate food—typically isn't likely to help anyone. Assuming we're not exploiting others, refusing to appreciate good things doesn't mean others' lives will somehow get better. In fact, we can trust that people who don't enjoy our material wealth, who grieve in ways we don't, still have their own pleasures in life. And when we recognize that the most pleasurable things in life—like healthy relationships, laughter, a job well done, sabbath rest, a good night's sleep, soul-deep connections, living with purpose, learning—abound, we realize that even when others face obstacles that keep them from enjoying these pleasures, our enjoyment of them doesn't limit their availability to the rest of humanity. We can live in a way that celebrates their abundance, abandoning the scarcity mindset that suggests our enjoyment must come at the expense of someone else.

Pleasure is temporary for all of us. And it fits nicely into the unsatisfied life when we recognize and accept that reality. Denying ourselves a happy moment is a great tragedy—that moment will never repeat itself. We were created with capacity to enjoy beauty, peace, warmth, surprises, familiarity, food, sex, sleep, human connection, novelty, artistry, quality, and so much more. Living intentionally unsatisfied does not mean we have to deny our attraction to these things. It simply means we neither expect an exclusively pleasurable life nor expect more from pleasure than God intended for it to give us.

PLEASURE SWEETENS OUR LIVES

It's not difficult to see how pleasure, properly enjoyed, enriches our lives. It eases tension, provides relief, lifts our mood, offers hope, encourages us, builds our strength, binds us to one another, makes us more optimistic, gives us sustaining memories, brings us balance, keeps us healthy, helps us see things from a new perspective, reminds us to count our blessings and thank God, helps us connect with our creativity, teaches us more about God's character, helps us better understand the way God has made us, and gives us a small glimpse of what life was intended to be.

We can find many places in Scripture that affirm and celebrate enjoyment of life's good gifts. Jesus frequently ate with his disciples and with others, including wealthy and prominent people who must have served lavish meals (Luke 5:27-33). The Song of Songs is a sensuous and extravagant celebration of love and intimacy. After God parted the waters of the Red Sea to save his people from Pharaoh's chariots, Miriam led the women of Israel in an eruption of dancing, playing music, and singing in joy and praise (Exodus 15:19-21). If God frowned on enjoyment of life, he would have brought his people to a dry, monotonous land where stimulation would be limited; instead he led them to "a good and spacious land, a land flowing with milk and honey" (Exodus 3:8).

The wisdom of Proverbs and Ecclesiastes, and the poetry of Psalms, assure us of the value of various types of pleasure, including happiness, godly friendship, the joys that come in simply being friends with God, and enjoying what God gives (see Psalm 133:1-2; Proverbs 16:11; 17:22; Ecclesiastes 5:18-19).

The apostle Paul, who had few recorded New Testament moments to enjoy what most of us might call pleasure, wrote of spiritual and mental enjoyment: "Rejoice in the Lord always. I will say it again: Rejoice!" (Philippians 4:4).

Pleasure is part of what it means to live in the world God made, part of what it means to be human. And it's part of what it looks like to live intentionally unsatisfied. In a life revolving around the now and the not yet of ultimate satisfaction through Jesus, pleasure is not the center of the universe, but it's a warm planet in the solar system. Thank God it's part of our world.

PLEASURE'S LIMITATIONS

So if pleasure is a good thing, and good for us, why are we so nervous about it and so often warned against enjoying it?

Well, let's acknowledge that some people have a natural aversion to enjoying anything. I'm reminded of some of the older church folks from my childhood, people who felt children's laughter was a violation of sacred space, who frowned on going back for seconds at the potluck, who scowled at anyone who dared tap a toe to the music in a church service. From where I sat, such people seemed joyless, even miserable, and determined to inflict their own sense of austere gloom on everyone around them. They seemed certain pleasure had no place in the Christian life.

The primary reason pleasure has a sketchy reputation is that it's frequently abused. And when people abuse anything, they cause damage. We hurt other people, destroy ourselves, and pollute the source of pleasure itself. When people elevate pleasure above love, respect, faithfulness, self-control, or any other virtue, it transforms into a monster. When we enjoy our pleasures outside the bounds of God's laws for human behavior, it eventually turns to ash. When we live for it, eventually we find ourselves slaves to it. When we worship pleasure or ask it to rule our lives, it crumbles like any other false god.

It's so tempting to try to coax out of pleasure more than it can give us. We try to make it last forever, when its nature is always temporary. We try to make it our natural state, when it isn't intended to be that. Pleasure isn't good for us when we try to make it the only thing we experience. Like the Velveteen Rabbit, it is made real through the hardships of life, when it coexists with longing and sorrow, pain and restlessness, boredom, vulnerability, and anger. Pleasure simply cannot bear the full weight of our existence. And by its very nature, it never lasts long. In fact, the longer it lasts, in many cases, the less enjoyment we find in it.

Before my husband and I moved to Alaska, we had seen the northern lights a couple of times when they were visible as far south as Chicago. But this was nothing compared to the lights we saw in Alaska. Once the nights were dark enough in the fall, the lights made frequent appearances, and they were so much more spectacular than what we had seen before. But most of the time they were one color—green—and after a while we got used to them and the green ones didn't warrant much more than a comment.

One night, at a youth retreat at a Christian camp, the adult leaders snuck out to try to see the lights, which were supposed to be out that night. And sure enough, in this place away from all traces of city lights, on a perfectly clear night, we saw them put on a more glorious show than I can possibly describe—and they were nothing like the versions we had become so accustomed to farther south and among the lights of modern civilization. They were straight overhead, filling the whole sky with every color of the rainbow. They undulated slowly, swirling above our heads, glowing brighter and brighter, and suddenly they exploded in a frenetic dance for a few moments before settling again into their slow sway.

Spontaneously, we did our own dance. We clapped and cheered and jumped around like the enthusiastic audience we were. We truly couldn't help ourselves. We were inspired to show our appreciation for the lights and our praise to the one who created them.

It was an incredible experience in its own right, but part of what makes this a precious memory is that it happened only once. Despite seeing the lights many times before and since that night, for us this glorious display was a once-in-a-lifetime experience. If we had seen them in that kind of brilliance ten times, the eleventh time wouldn't have looked as good as the first. In fact, after enough light shows, eventually this spectacular display would not have seemed spectacular—it would have found the same status as the all-green version we usually saw from our home.

The same thing happens when we are repeatedly exposed to pleasure of any kind. We may still enjoy it, but unless we find new ways to appreciate it, it won't thrill us the way it once did. Pleasure is fleeting, circumstantial, and partly based on novelty. When we can't find pleasure anymore and we insist on more and more escalation, pleasure is beginning to consume us.

In 2011, Gallup published research showing the optimal income for happiness: $75,000. I don't know whether that number should be adjusted for inflation, but at the time they claimed, "People with an annual household income of $75,000 are about as happy as anyone gets." Perhaps the most interesting implication of this finding was that people who made more than $75,000 weren't any happier, regardless of how high their income was. In fact, they pointed out that "other research suggests that wealthy people don't take as much pleasure in actual pleasure as do poor people. In one test, social researchers primed some test subjects to feel rich and found that the 'wealthy' subjects didn't enjoy luxury chocolate as much as the control group, the 'non-wealthy,' did." It makes sense. When you know you can have luxury chocolate anytime you want it, you probably won't derive as much pleasure from eating it as someone who is trying it for the first time, or for whom it truly is a luxury. Sadly, many have sought satisfaction in pleasure, and ultimately they have found themselves less satisfied than before.

Many people cause destruction for themselves and others in their quest for pleasure. Some people will do anything to experience pleasure. This is a sign of worship—an unholy reverence that treats pleasure as an object of worship, high above all else, with no sacrifice too great. Many have made it their god, placing it in a role it can't live up to. When we worship pleasure, build our lives around it, expect it to satisfy, or barter for it with what is better (love, kindness, moderation, wisdom, health), it betrays us with its weakness. It bends under our weight, crumbles, and turns to dust. In our desire to make it fully satisfy us, it exposes new levels of dissatisfaction.

Pleasure makes a wonderful gift—and a terrible god.

A WORD ABOUT HAPPINESS

Pleasure takes many forms—physical, mental, spiritual, emotional. We have many words for emotional pleasure, including *elation, euphoria, delight, bliss,* and *good cheer.* But perhaps the best overarching word for this category of emotion is *happiness.* And boy, do we place heavy expectations on the shoulders of happiness—far more than it can ever meet. After all, the American life is supposed to be about the pursuit of happiness, right? Happiness, like other forms of pleasure, is one element of a good life. It is not the point of life.

I know I'm going to alienate someone with this admission, but I'm going to stick my neck out and confess that I wasn't "clapping along" to Pharrell Williams's song "Happy" back when it was the most popular (and ubiquitous) song of 2014. It's a fine song with an appealing sound, and it seems to make many people, well, happy. But I just couldn't get into it because the lyrics sound so much like a philosophy of life that has left many people bereft.

I'm a fairly hopeful person, and I absolutely believe in God's goodness. I also love to laugh. And I definitely love to be happy. But I can't say I believe "happiness is the truth." Oddly enough, this lyric makes me sad because it presents an accurate summary of a worldview many people are hoping will bring them ultimate satisfaction. Building a life around their own happiness is the best they can come up with, and I can't blame them. But I know it's not enough.

As with other forms of pleasure, happiness is not a bad thing. In fact, it's a good and wonderful thing. But again, it's inadequate to sustain us as a reason for living or the truth around which our lives are built. Happiness is an important element of satisfaction, but it's no antidote to lack of satisfaction. People who have experienced a lot of happiness can be as miserable as anyone else. People who are happy one moment can be devastated the next. And for those who spend their lives chasing happiness, it will almost certainly lead to disappointment and disillusionment. Like all forms of pleasure, it's fleeting, highly circumstantial, and subject to abuse.

So is the pursuit of happiness an empty chase or, worse, a wicked pastime? As with other forms of pleasure, many of us are confused about whether it's okay to pursue happiness. Maybe it's because we see happiness as an all-or-nothing proposition: either I'm only happy or I'm only unhappy. My life is either a happy one or an unhappy one. It's easy to believe that enjoying happiness requires banishing negative emotions. But we can experience happy moments in a sad life, and vice versa. We can laugh and cry at the same time. We have an incredible capacity for coexisting emotions if we're willing and courageous enough to open to them. Happiness serves us well when we recognize its limitations.

Instead, we are so often tempted to make happiness our god, our paramount goal in life, our stand-in for truth. Happiness is the normal state of being for exactly no one. When we consider it our only acceptable emotional circumstance, we miss out on the wealth of learning, depth of being, and extent of growth available in the majority of our experiences. In fact, like other forms of pleasure, happiness offers diminishing returns. It has more power when it's not the only thing we know. I believe happiness is a good thing to pursue and enjoy when we can, but we must not let it displace our capacity for other emotions and override our sense of mission and purpose, which are intended to transcend our emotions and circumstances.

Like the proverbial bluebird, happiness will come and go. So when it visits you, go ahead and be happy! And when it doesn't, look forward to the times when you will enjoy its presence again. In the meantime, get comfortable with the wider range of emotions that fly in, settle, and sing their own songs in your unsatisfied life.

PLEASURE IN THE UNSATISFIED LIFE

How do we embrace both healthy pleasure and unsatisfaction at the same time? We follow the advice of Ecclesiastes 7:14 and keep pleasure in its proper place: "When times are good, be happy; but when times are bad, consider this: God has made the one as well as the other."

The following strategies can help us embrace both pleasure and unsatisfaction.

Distinguish pleasure and happiness from joy. In C. S. Lewis's *Surprised by Joy*, he wrote of

> an unsatisfied desire which is itself more desirable than any other satisfaction. I call it Joy, which is here a technical term and must be sharply distinguished both from Happiness and Pleasure. Joy (in my sense) has indeed one characteristic, and one only, in common with them; the fact that anyone who has experienced it will want it again. . . . I doubt whether anyone who has tasted it would ever, if both were in his power, exchange it for all the pleasures in the world. But then Joy is never in our power and Pleasure often is.

I'm intrigued by his definition of joy as an unfulfilled longing that is more pleasurable than the fulfillment of pleasure. Others frequently define joy as a deeper, more stable cousin of happiness, spiritually based and not shaken by circumstances. This rings true, but what if joy is more than an experience—what if it's a glimmer of desire for the unseen, for which we lack the capacity even to thirst because it's so foreign to our limited abilities here and now? This kind of God-given anticipation can sustain us when absolutely no form of pleasure, or even spiritually assuring words, can speak to our soul. Welcoming God's gift of joy in your life is completely different from pursuing pleasure, and it's completely compatible with unsatisfaction. Perhaps it is a form of satisfaction.

Let pleasure live alongside the harsh realities of life. The grim truths about life don't have to overshadow the graces. You don't have to pretend only good exists before you can appreciate what is good. Enjoy the beauty of a tree, even though you know that somewhere trees are being chopped down. Enjoy the pleasure of loved ones' company even though you know they will be lost to you someday. Go ahead and enjoy happy days and happy moments without waiting for the anvil to fall from the sky. Enjoy good things without feeling guilty others don't have them (unless your having them is actually depriving others).

Tell yourself the truth about both positive and negative realities. We can allow ourselves to appreciate the positive realities while still living with full acknowledgment of the negative. And be realistic about relationships. Take pleasure in knowing other people, giving and taking, without expecting any of these relationships to give you all that you want or need. Remember that the most authentic and lasting forms of pleasure come from loving God and loving others.

Engage in worship. Rejoice in the Lord always (Philippians 4:4)! Direct your pleasure God's way, expressing your delight in who God is, what he does, and what he has made. Find pleasure in loving God's Word and in prayer and fellowship with him. Remain grateful to God at all times. It's amazing how seeing something as a gift and expressing gratitude for it can keep our hearts open and help us retain a taste for the simple.

Let pleasure ignite in you a longing for something greater. Pleasure in this world is a shadow of what is more real, truer, and purer in the world to come. Relationships, laughter, moments of intimacy, the gratification of making someone else happy—all point toward the unbroken fellowship of people who have been remade as they should be. Food, beautiful days, beautiful music and other artistic expressions, those wonderful and very fleeting moments of feeling worry-free and insecurity-free—all are pointing us toward what will one day belong to all who accept God's ultimate gift. Rather than seek satisfaction in these lesser pleasures, let them sharpen your appetite for what's better.

Keep happiness and pleasure in their place. Avoid expecting happiness and pleasure to satisfy you, demanding they deliver more than momentary goodness, worshiping them or building your life around them, or paying too much for them (trading them for people you love, time you'll never get back, your health, someone else's well-being, your soul). Remember that memory and anticipation are their own forms of pleasure, and when we exercise moderation we keep these things alive. Choose to look for happiness and delight in places where they're not obvious. Refuse to believe the lies that lure us toward shiny objects. Most of the things that glitter in this world aren't gold. Stay away from soul traps. Some "pleasures" won't bring pleasure at all.

When we don't ask more of it than it can deliver, pleasure is a wonderful gift. When we choose to live unsatisfied, we don't have to choose displeasure. But like anything we abuse, pleasure will turn against us when we make it an idol. So enjoy the good things God gives you! But don't believe any promises of complete satisfaction. Instead, remain unsatisfied as pleasure fills its appropriate place in your life.

Blessings of the Unsatisfied Life:
THE BLESSING OF VISION

Unsatisfaction helps us develop and pursue a motivating vision for a world better than the one we live in. That vision encourages us to reach for a higher standard. This is important in both the present and the future. People who carry a vision for that better world can't really settle for life as we know it. The ones who lose that vision convince themselves this is as good as we can hope for.

When I was in high school, I attended a school that was racially diverse, although the different racial groups did not always mix freely. My experience at church, though, was entirely different. While my family lived in the city, we went to church in the suburbs, and almost everyone in the congregation was white.

On one occasion, my family went with a group of people from the church to serve at a homeless shelter in the city. On the same evening, a group from a predominantly African American church was there serving as well. I remember feeling profoundly uncomfortable as both groups sat in the mission's cafeteria at the end of the evening, enjoying a time of fellowship and talking about the experience—within our own groups. Here we were, two churches serving in the name of Jesus, sitting on opposite sides of the room and acting as if the other did not exist.

I remember squirming in my seat, looking at the other group and feeling I should break the ice. Part of me (I think it was the part of me that was listening to the Holy Spirit) wanted to get up, walk across the room, and say hello. To forge a connection with our brothers and sisters in Christ. I had a sense that other people wanted that connection and didn't know how to make it happen, and that they would follow me. Among the group I was with, I felt uniquely qualified to take the lead. After all, I was a teenager, and people expect them to do reckless things. And I was comfortable with an everyday multicultural experience that most people in my church did not have and probably had never had. But the rest of me was afraid I would be dismissed or ignored, afraid no one else would follow and I would find myself awkwardly unsure of what to say or do, afraid to challenge a state of affairs that, on the surface, seemed to be working for everyone else.

Inertia won. I stayed in my seat. And so did everyone else. And that moment of decision has stuck with me ever since. That moment of choosing cowardice over obedience to the Spirit produced a sense of failure and disappointment that remains vivid for me. As with everyone else there, I chose to be satisfied with the way things were even though God was calling me to be unsatisfied—and to take action as a result. More than once in the intervening years, my unsatisfaction with that experience has motivated me to take some risks in pursuit of a vision of a stronger and more unified body of Christ.

Christians aren't the only ones with a vision for a better world; everyone wants life to be better for themselves and for others. But we don't all agree on how to pursue that vision (or exactly what it might look like). As Christians we acknowledge we do not have the power to fix the fundamental problem with this world: human sin. We know we're in need of redemption—and ultimately a re-making. Yet we aren't supposed to settle for the world as we know it. We are supposed to spread "the fragrance of Christ" (2 Corinthians 2:15-17) in this life even as we live in hope of the next. Unsatisfaction helps us keep our eyes on both.

It can also help us notice and respond to ways we can make life better for other people. There's no reason we should be satisfied with life on earth as we know it. Followers of Christ who give up on the world have lost touch with the heart of God, who has never abandoned us to the fate we chose. Disease, violence, terrorism, poverty, pain, and suffering of all kinds are consequences of human sin. Human efforts cannot cure these ills, but they can and should ease suffering, bring healing, and stand up for good. As people indebted to grace, Jesus' followers are under obligation to help. As people of hope, we have no excuse for writing anyone off as a lost cause. When we remain intimate with our unsatisfaction, we expand our own capacity for hope on behalf of everyone.

At the same time, as "foreigners and exiles" in this world (1 Peter 2:11) our unsatisfaction can keep us looking beyond this life with a vision for what God will ultimately do to redeem his creation. Our hunger for perfect justice is rooted in our awareness of God. Our desire for safety and security is planted in our longing for his presence. Those longings are good. And ultimately our vision of a world beyond this one can fuel our efforts to live a life worthy of our calling (Ephesians 4:1) here and now.

As C. S. Lewis wrote,

> If we consider the unblushing promises of reward and the staggering nature of the rewards promised in the gospels, it would seem that Our Lord finds our desires not too strong, but too weak. We are half-hearted creatures, fooling about with drink and sex and ambition when infinite joy is offered us, like an ignorant child who wants to go on making mud pies in a slum because he cannot imagine what is meant by the offer of a holiday at the sea. We are far too easily pleased.

Let's keep our standards high, refusing to be lulled by the flawed fare of what even a faith-filled life in this world can give us. True faith is hungry; it will not be satisfied by what we can experience here and now. Unsatisfaction reminds us what we were made for and keeps it in our view. It keeps us straining toward it, like plants that bend toward the light streaming in through a window. God wants us to long for more! He wants more for us; if our hearts beat in time with his, they will never lose touch with the God-given vision of the full reconciliation of God and humanity—the day when we will stand in the very presence of our Creator.

EXERCISES

- Look into local organizations that are working to improve life in your community. Contact at least one to see how you can get involved in supporting them.

- How does your own sense of unsatisfaction help you visualize a better world? Take some time to create something that represents what you long for: a written description, a drawing or painting, a collage, a Pinterest board, a chart or graph, a song, or something else. Then consider this: How would your life have to change if you were going to live in a world like that one? Once you have your answer, start taking steps to pursue those changes in your own life.

- None of us is capable of saving the world, and even all of us put together, doing our very best work, can't overcome the destructive power of rebellion against our Creator. But as the community of people representing Christ in this world, the church offers a kind of hope found nowhere else. Read Matthew 5:13-16 and agree with Jesus' own vision for the role his people should play in society.

Embrace Contentment

8

When I was a child, my family moved several times. By the time I reached ninth grade, we had lived in nine different places (including a year in Switzerland while my parents attended language school in preparation for a missionary career that never materialized). We stayed put through my high school years, and after I graduated I went away to college and lived in a dorm room for a few years. In the middle of my senior year I got married and moved into an apartment with my husband. A year later we moved one thousand miles away . . . and kept moving. By the time we moved into the house I'm sitting in now, more than eleven years ago, we had been married for twelve years and lived in twelve different places (if you count the two weeks we spent living in a camper in someone's driveway in Alaska, waiting for our rental house to be ready). I was in my midthirties, and I had never spent more than five years living in any one place.

The school-age moves were hard on me, but I'm thankful for the skills they taught me, making me more adaptable, better at making friends, and more adept at letting go than I might have been otherwise. But they also made me restless. About seven years ago, when we were approaching five years of living here, I was tremendously restless, itching to move on to somewhere new. It just felt like time to go—five years was my limit! But we didn't move, and I began to get used to the idea of staying put for a while. It's been interesting to see how much a place, and the people in it, change over ten years, and to feel a sense of ownership and belonging in a community.

I'm settled where I am for now, but I'm restless by nature—not simply for the sake of moving on, but because I am hooked on the possibilities in a new place: the fresh start, the opportunity to begin again, learn from my mistakes, and do it better the next time. Contentment is a true challenge for me; I definitely have not mastered it. My personality and temperament tell me that if something good is going to happen I'd better make it happen. They also tell me that one of the worst things I could do is sit back and let life pass me by, or risk going through life without making a positive mark on the world. And in general, because I tend toward perfectionism, I'm very much attracted to the idea that I can finally get it right.

But I can't really get it right—and neither can you. Contentment requires us to embrace this truth, among other things, and this kind of acceptance is where contentment and unsatisfaction meet. When we learn to stop asking the world for more than it can give us, and stop asking ourselves to live up to impossible standards, we begin our journey toward both embracing unsatisfaction and living with contentment.

At first glance, contentment and unsatisfaction may look like an odd couple. How can I be content if I'm unsatisfied? But they really do get along well. The key is in understanding that contentment, as a discipline, does not demand perfection; if it did, it would work itself out of a job. If our lives were truly complete, there would be no need for us to be intentionally content with what we have, who we are, or what our circumstances are. When we someday return to the world we were made for and achieve total satisfaction in a fully restored relationship with God, all our needs and desires will be fully gratified. Contentment will be obsolete. For now, contentment is necessary precisely because we are unsatisfied.

Remember, being intentionally unsatisfied is not the same as being dissatisfied. When we choose to live unsatisfied, we remain open to our longing for what is far better than what we have, while we abandon the quest to find or manufacture it for ourselves. We embrace current reality in light of our future reality. We accept what we cannot change, knowing someday it will change dramatically. Contentment represents a similar act of acceptance. It requires us to embrace what is rather than chase the charms of a life that isn't ours, and perhaps isn't even possible here and now. If we are seeking full satisfaction in this life, we actively work against our efforts at contentment. By contrast, contentment plays an important role in the unsatisfied life.

CONTENTMENT DEFINED

When I talk about contentment, what exactly am I talking about? Contentment is an ease of mind that comes with setting aside our yearning and striving for something more or different.

Contentment isn't a reflection of our circumstances or any part of the external world. Rather, it's an internal state of affairs that reflects the condition of our mind and spirit. Seventeenth-century Puritan preacher Thomas Watson put it this way: "Contentment lies within a man, in the heart; and the way to be comfortable, is not by having our barns filled—but our minds quiet."

Richard A. Swenson calls contentment a secret path to freedom:

> Freedom from wanting more than is good for us. Freedom to wish blessing on everyone we meet without the slightest tinge of envy. Freedom to redefine wealth and possessions in biblical rather than cultural terms. Freedom to gladly surrender our strife and have it replaced by His rest. Freedom to be biblically authentic in an age of financially-forced compromises. Freedom to understand that one heart, inhabited by Christ, is enough to take on the world's opinion machine.

An important part of defining contentment is distinguishing it from some of the things it's not:

- Contentment is not resignation—just accepting things as they are because you believe they can't be better or because you feel helpless. For example, when I started writing this book I was recovering from spinal-fusion surgery. I felt miserable, I was in pain, I was limited in what I could do, and I was at the mercy of people who were willing to help. There was a chance my vertebrae would not fully heal from the surgery, and I knew the experience had permanently altered my body, no matter what happened. No procedure could truly undo the injury I had sustained. But I could be content in actively working toward recovery, knowing my rest and my dependence on other people increased the chances that I would get better. So I put myself in the hands of my doctors and nurses, my husband, and other people who were willing to take care of me. This was not the same as giving up.

- Contentment is not apathy—being fine with everything simply because you really don't care.

- Contentment is not delusion or self-induced blindness—sticking your head in the sand or blinding yourself with palliative sayings like "everything happens for a reason" and "it will all work out in the end."

- Contentment is not Pollyannaish optimism—believing bad circumstances are always good, nothing is a tragedy, and life has no room for grief.

In contentment we can care deeply, live competently, and courageously face life as it really is. We can recognize the faint tracings of a hidden and wonderful plan that overrules all our schemes and dreams. Contentment is refusing to convert our need for God into lust for a new house, car, or relationship. It's refusing to trade the indestructible for something we could lose tomorrow, refusing to believe someone else's life ought to be ours. Contentment is independent from our circumstances. In contentment we can appreciate pain for its benefits. We can live peacefully with a heart that knows it has not yet been satisfied and remains open to longing for what is to come. It is the mindset that can sing "It Is Well with My Soul" when it looks as if we have lost everything.

CONTENTMENT IN THE CHRISTIAN LIFE

On the Myers-Briggs Type Indicator personality inventory, I am an INFJ. Among other things, this means I struggle with idealistic perfectionism. Here's a quote from the website 16 Personalities, describing INFJs like me: "INFJs are all but defined by their pursuit of ideals. While this is a wonderful quality in many ways, an ideal situation is not always possible—in politics, in business, in romance—and INFJs too often drop or ignore healthy and productive situations and relationships, always believing there might be a better option down the road." Does this sound like a description of someone who might not be adept at contentment? It is.

And while striving for perfection, or at least a better option, is a hallmark part of my personality, contentment is a significant topic addressed in Scripture, and clearly it's part of our calling as Christians. Both a lack of contentment and a failure to look to God as the source of provision can be at the root of what causes people to turn away from God and his ways. So much so that a wise man named Agur son of Jakeh made a counterintuitive request of God which I need to learn to pray, immortalized in Proverbs 30:8-9:

> Keep falsehood and lies far from me;
>> give me neither poverty nor riches,
>> but give me only my daily bread.
> Otherwise, I may have too much and disown you
>> and say, "Who is the LORD?"
> Or I may become poor and steal,
>> and so dishonor the name of my God.

This is a compelling picture of contentment. And in a sense, this is a prayer for unsatisfaction—for the fulfillment of only immediate needs, not the neutralization of need itself. This is because unsatisfaction—not dissatisfaction, desperation, or superabundance—provides the best environment for contentment to grow. It makes sense to pray for only our daily bread. Having only what we need is good for our spiritual condition if we embrace its benefits and learn to be content rather than constantly strive for more.

When someone asked Jesus to arbitrate a family dispute, he dismissed the issue's significance and confronted the covetousness behind the man's request: "Someone in the crowd said to him, 'Teacher, tell my brother to divide the inheritance with me.' Jesus replied, 'Man, who appointed me a judge or an arbiter between you?' Then he said to them, 'Watch out! Be on your guard against all kinds of greed; life does not consist in an abundance of possessions'" (Luke 12:13-15). One of the things I hear in Jesus' response to this man is disgust with the idea that people would come to him, the highly disruptive source of abundant and eternal life who is making all things new, and ask for the means to get more comfortable where they were. That disgruntled brother missed the point as profoundly as we do today. Like him, we sometimes come to Jesus with the request that our lives be so full of blessing that we no longer feel our need. But Jesus wants us to remain aware of our need for him and what he will someday lavish on us. In the meantime, we can be content with what we have while acknowledging we are not fully satisfied by it. We are content while we continue to be in need.

Although we like to believe God is concerned with making his people's circumstances as happy and snag-free as possible, his priorities are very different from ours. In the words of my friend Dr. Stephen Grcevich, one hurtful result of bad theology can be that "we fail to recognize that it may be OK with God if we struggle or suffer so long as it accomplishes HIS purposes." When God works through things like suffering, pain, and disappointment—as he often does—we need to learn to be content in a world where we will not be satisfied.

Let me acknowledge that we should not be content with everything. The world we live in is undeniably broken and full of tragedy. None of us is who we were made to be, and we're always in need of growth and correction. We should not be content to overlook injustice, ignore the effects of rebellion against God, or allow people to suffer when we can do something to help. We should not be content with our own level of goodness at any given point. Pastor Bill Hybels's book *Holy Discontent* speaks of a kind of discontentment that causes us to rise up and take action in Jesus' name. This passionate pursuit of righteousness is not the opposite of Christian contentment; it's the opposite of apathy or inertia. When I advocate for contentment in this chapter, I'm not talking about complacency.

True contentment does not cause us to stop caring about the world; it enables us to care for others when our own circumstances aren't what we would choose for ourselves. It does not stunt our growth; it enriches our lives. It halts our constant striving for more, calms our appetites, helps us see the good in where we are, draws our eyes off ourselves and our own comfort so we can live missionally and with God-given purpose. True contentment does not wait for full satisfaction; it engages most powerfully when we recognize our hunger and thirst and helps us focus on the provision made for both. Contentment helps us gracefully stay where we are. It also helps us make transitions and adapt to new places and situations.

Contentment is a beautiful capstone to the pursuits I discussed in the previous three chapters: it helps us find fulfillment where God has placed us instead of pursuing more and greater; it helps us find meaning and make an impact where we are instead of always trying to change our circumstances; it helps us find pleasure in life as we know it. We have far more to gain from contentment than from all the wealth and happy circumstances we are so easily convinced will make our lives enjoyable. We will find more freedom in a state of contentment than we ever will in all our efforts to fill a void within us with shadows of things to come.

THE POISON OF COMPLAINING

Complaining fuels discontentment.

Complaining is different from noticing problems and constructively pointing to them, sharing ideas for improvement, or making plans for positive change. Mere complaining is a lazy choice, one that's most comfortable with an assumption of powerlessness that may not reflect reality. But we are never truly powerless to choose how we will respond to our circumstances. As Thomas Watson advised, "Would we have comfort in our lives? We may have it if we will. A Christian may carve out whatever condition he will to himself. Why do you complain of your troubles? It is not trouble which troubles—but discontentment. It is not outward affliction which can make the life of a Christian sad; a contented mind would sail above these waters—but when discontent gets into the heart, then it is disquieted and sinks." Eventually complaining will embitter our hearts against the places where they might otherwise find a creative medium or a sweet sense of God's presence. It will keep us from contentment every time.

Numbers 11 gives us a horrifying demonstration of how God reacted when his ancient people were looking for absolute satisfaction of their cravings. God gave them miraculous provision along with an opportunity for trust, but because they were focused on satisfaction, they missed the opportunity for contentment and instead complained about what God had given them. Verse 1 of that chapter tells us, "The people complained about their hardships in the hearing of the Lord, and when he heard them his anger was aroused." In fact, he sent fire to their camp, and some of the people were burned. But in spite of this warning, the people of Israel soon began complaining again, this time specifically about their food.

They were on their way to the land God had promised to give them, and they had some other people traveling with them, non-Israelites who had left Egypt with them. The NIV calls these people "the rabble." The rabble had a contagious lack of gratitude: "The rabble with them began to crave other food, and again the Israelites started wailing and said, 'If only we had meat to eat! We remember the fish we ate in Egypt at no cost—also the cucumbers, melons, leeks, onions and garlic. But now we have lost our appetite; we never see anything but this manna!'" (Numbers 11:4-6).

The thing was, God had miraculously provided food where there was no food. He gave them enough for each day, and he was teaching them to depend on him and to be his people. He was lovingly caring for them as he led them toward a land of their own and a new life as an independent nation under his protection. No, it wasn't a life of luxury—but it was exactly what they needed. And here they were complaining about the food and actually longing for the good old days when they were living in slavery and their food was available "at no cost." Complaints about the food amounted to rejection of God himself and his plan for them.

So after hearing from God, Moses told them they would have a sickening overabundance of meat. The ground around the camp was blanketed with quail, and the people gathered more than they could possibly enjoy. But the consequences of complaining didn't stop there. Soon, "while the meat was still between their teeth and before it could be consumed" (Numbers 11:33), a plague struck and killed those whose cravings led them to ingratitude. These people had lost sight of the goodness from God and complained, destroying contentment. They expected satisfaction on their terms and, as so many still do, turned against God when he didn't deliver it, despite all the ways he was guiding, feeding, and blessing them. Rather than activate contentment in their unsatisfied state, they chose to embitter themselves into dissatisfaction.

Should the Israelites have been truly satisfied with manna in the wilderness? No, I don't believe so. I believe God wanted them to desire the Promised Land that was intended for them, where he was leading them. I believe he wanted them to look forward to the place where they would settle and enjoy a variety of good foods. But along the way they had the opportunity to be content with what God gave them, knowing it was more than they deserved. Like all of us, they could have chosen contentment despite feeling unsatisfied. But also like many of us, they felt satisfaction had to come first.

I don't think it's accidental or insignificant that the text tells us the complaining started with the rabble who were traveling with the Israelites. These folks were a bad influence, and their spirit was contagious. Complaining is still contagious, and we now know, not only from experience but through science, that being around complaining changes our brains in negative ways. Author Trevor Blake claims, "If you're pinned in a corner for too long listening to someone being negative, you're more likely to behave that way as well." Whether we're complaining or listening to someone else do it, it damages the hippocampus in our brains, the critically important center of emotion and memory.

And if listening to others complain is harmful, our own complaining is even more so. In general, the thought patterns we indulge become the ones we are most likely to employ in the future. Like other complex systems, the brain is prone to shortcuts. The neural pathways we use grow easier to access as the relevant neurons in our brains form shortcuts by growing closer together and forming secure connections. So as we indulge in complaining, we encourage the formation of our own mental shortcuts to negative thinking. The more we complain, the more we want to complain. Over time, it becomes easier and easier for us to see what's wrong with the world around us and harder to see what's right.

I've certainly experienced this in my own life. While I'm growing in my ability to respond in a reasonable way and to be judicious in my remarks, I have sometimes been the complainer who led everyone else into negativity—more often than I'm comfortable admitting. When I become unhappy with a circumstance or situation, I'm unlikely to stay quiet about it unless I see that it's clearly in my own best interest to do so. So I am guilty of spreading this particular poison through classrooms, organizations, church groups, and workplaces.

This is one reason people so often speak of the power of staying positive. While positive thinking may not have all the powers attributed to it over the years, it does have a strong beneficial impact on us—and on the people around us. Negativity has similar potential, but with destructive results.

So take care to avoid complaining! And if you are waiting for satisfaction before choosing contentment, no need to wait. Contentment can live well in an unsatisfied soul.

UNSATISFIED CONTENTMENT

How does contentment fit into the unsatisfied life? Let's look at Philippians 4:13 for a clue. Right after Paul claims to have learned the secret to contentment regardless of his circumstances, he writes this: "I can do all this through him who gives me strength." At least, this is how the NIV translates the verse, dealing a blow to all those who have chosen to interpret it as a carte blanche Jesus-empowered promise of superhuman ability.

At first glance, pulled out of context and quoted from the King James Version or from the 1984 version of the NIV, "I can do everything through him who gives me strength," it's easy to interpret this verse to mean we can do anything because we have Jesus on our side, making us stronger than we would be on our own. We use it to boost our confidence, and sometimes, if we're honest, what we really mean is, "God will empower me to make my dreams come true." "I can do whatever I want to do, and I'll be successful because God will make sure it happens." "I can beat the competition because God makes me stronger than them." It's a great verse for reinforcing a self-centric worldview, printing on bumper stickers, and quoting in personal pep talks. But these are gross misuses of this verse. As Inigo Montoya might say in *The Princess Bride*, "You keep using that word. I do not think it means what you think it means." We don't get to pull verses out of context and claim them for our personal slogans to make us feel like winners.

In fact, embracing this verse should be a sober exercise. Paul's confidence in writing these words came at serious cost. For Paul, "all this" referred to verse 12, in which Paul mentioned his experience with an impressive variety of circumstances: "to be in need . . . to have plenty . . . well fed or hungry . . . living in plenty or in want." Paul could do all *circumstances* through the strength supplied by Christ. His confidence came from his history of suffering. As Paul wrote this very letter to the church in Philippi, he was living as a prisoner.

Yes, we can also do "all this" through Christ, who gives us strength. But the "all this" to which God calls us may not make any of our dreams come true. It will not satisfy us or make us perfectly safe and comfortable in this life. It almost certainly will involve some kind of suffering. The consistency of Christ's presence, and the experience of drawing on his strength, is the true secret to contentment.

It's one thing to say that Christ will strengthen us for contentment; it's another thing to seek and cooperate with that process. Because it goes against our nature, embracing contentment requires discipline. We have choices to make. Here are some specific practices that can help us foster contentment while remaining unsatisfied.

Look for strength outside yourself. I'm sorry to break it to you, but you really don't have what it takes. If you walk in your own strength, sooner or later something will break you, if it hasn't already. The only one capable of putting you back together will be the one who made you in the first place. Why not draw your strength from him before you can no longer deny that you need it? Go ahead and submit to God's authority and wisdom. There is no point in resisting, and why would you want to fight the will of the one who knows everything and loves you more than you can fathom? He may want you to stay where you are; he might take you somewhere you didn't even know was on the map. Ask God for the faith to truly believe him—look to God's revelation of himself through

Scripture, and believe what you find there. Look around you for evidence of God's goodness, redemption, and hope. You don't need a change in circumstances to find God with you.

Feed the right appetites. Look back at chapter five and review the discussion of values. Get to know your own values so you can recognize how they fuel your desires. Consider what values are pulling you away from contentment and consider how you might honor them in a life-giving way without breeding discontentment. Indulge the desires that bring you true life and fulfillment, not the ones that just leave you wanting more of things that ultimately hurt you. Cultivate a taste for the good things God has given you. Practice a grateful attitude. Being thankful can completely change your perspective and help you see beauty in your circumstances and beyond them.

Be realistic. Start with realistic expectations. Contentment is within closer reach when you keep expectations for your life at a level that's actually attainable, when you expect others to be only what they are capable of being, and when you expect yourself to be only you. Don't be fooled by the illusory promises of the things and experiences that beckon you. Recognize the temporary and meaningless nature of much of what tempts you to lust or covet. Striving after the things you think will satisfy you only brings emptiness. Instead, make peace with unsatisfaction and find contentment.

Build your life around what really matters. In the well-known words of Charles Thomas Studd, "Only one life 'twill soon be past. Only what's done for Christ will last." Try taking your eyes off yourself. Sometimes we need to change our point of view. It's easy to believe we are the protagonists in our own stories, but we are all supporting characters in God's story. Focus on God's story and your place in it rather than the story you want to write for yourself, and your whole view of contentment will change as your desires shift.

Celebrate! The grass might be greener in your neighbor's yard, but that doesn't mean you would be happier over there. And it definitely doesn't mean you belong there. Focusing on what other people have, comparing ourselves with them, and striving to remake ourselves in their image are all poisonous activities that will eventually consume us from the inside. Celebration fuels contentment by helping us focus on what we have rather than what we don't. As with the people of ancient Israel, celebrations can help us stop to mark and remember what God has done. They also draw us into closer community with the people who celebrate with us.

If you believe satisfaction is a prerequisite for contentment, I challenge you to try embracing both unsatisfaction and contentment, just for one day, and see how the combination shifts your mindset. See how it pulls you toward your Creator. See how it draws your eyes away from yourself and your attempts at satisfaction. You may find a kind of peace you can't explain. You may find freedom—not the ultimate freedom that will come from being remade and placed in a fully redeemed world, but the kind of freedom that comes from contentedly looking forward to it.

We are a little like animals living in a zoo. If the zoo is a good one, the animals have all they need: nutritious food, relative safety, a peaceful place to sleep, medical care, probably even companionship. They have someone watching over them day and night. But for animals meant to live in the wild, this kind of life is not truly satisfying. While a world-weary creature, exhausted from hunting or eluding predators, may think a zoo would be the lap of luxury, these animals are not truly free. If they try to exercise all their desires, at some point they will run into the fence or the wall of glass that separates them from the world they were made for.

Like zoo animals, we can pace and paw at the glass and growl at the shortcomings of our habitat. Or we can acknowledge the limitations of the world we inhabit, accept that some of our longings will not be satisfied while we are here, and get to the business of contentment, knowing we will not be unconstrained until our keeper truly sets us free.

Contentment does not mean we must convince ourselves we already have all we long for. It doesn't mean we put away our longing for what is better. It means we rest in what we do have, knowing our hope is deferred, not dead. And that is the key to why both contentment and unsatisfaction make so much sense for followers of Christ: untamed, captivating, gratuitous hope. We know we will not be disappointed. We know true, complete freedom is coming.

Blessings of the Unsatisfied Life: THE BLESSING OF ANTICIPATION

While we live in this world, bound by time and its byproducts death and decay, unsatisfaction can keep us looking forward to the life beyond this one and help us keep that eternal perspective in view. Generally, satisfied people have little motivation to change their point of view. But unsatisfied people go looking for answers, for hope, for something better on the horizon. And unsatisfaction can lead us to find that "something better" in things that will last forever.

My youngest daughter is great at living in the moment. She's really fun to hang out with because her attention is on what she's doing, she cares about the person she's with, and she focuses on the present. And like many people who have her gift, she's not naturally inclined to make detailed plans for the future. But years ago she figured out that life is more fun if you have something to look forward to. So she started asking me when I tucked her in at night,

"What do we have to look forward to?" I would tell her what exciting things were on the calendar for the next couple of months, and she would smile and enjoy the anticipation as she settled in for sleep. Now that she's a teenager, she uses her own student planner and keeps track of the appointments and events that directly affect her. But still, almost every night at bedtime, she naturally turns her thoughts toward what's next and asks me, "What's happening tomorrow?" She may not plan far ahead, but like most of us she wants to know what's coming. And when something exciting is on the horizon, she goes to sleep with a smile on her face. Anticipation makes her life—and ours—sweeter.

If roughly eighty years of learning and forgetting, gaining and losing, succeeding and failing, laughing and crying were enough to satisfy us, we would not long for a world where death and decay are no longer on the march. We would have no reason to look beyond this life to the next.

When we numb ourselves with platitudes like "Death is just a part of life" and "It just wasn't meant to be," we can convince ourselves tragedies aren't important, grief and loss aren't bitter, and those who feel overwhelmed by such things are weak or flawed. We can lose touch with the feeling that anything should be different. We can convince ourselves that faith is supposed to function as a soothing tonic, keeping us from wanting—when God wants us to want what he intends to offer all who receive his gracious gifts.

In the Old Testament, three tribes of Israel showed how satisfaction can keep us from anticipating, or even accepting, what God offers us. Before God's chosen people took possession of the Promised Land, "a land flowing with milk and honey" (Exodus 13:5), they were encamped on the east side of the Jordan River. When the time came to move west, across the river and into the rich land God would give them, the tribe of Reuben, the tribe of Gad, and half the tribe of Manasseh wanted to stay where they

were. They were satisfied with what they knew on the east side of
the Jordan, where they had found land suitable for raising livestock.
Numbers 32:1-42 tells us of their conversation with Moses, when
they proposed to stay where they were. They agreed to fight
alongside the other tribes, to gain possession of the land, before
returning to their homes across the river. Moses accepted this pro-
posal, and God blessed their land. But they missed out on what
God had planned for them in the new place. They allowed their
sense of satisfaction to keep them from wanting and accepting
more from God—the Promised Land they hadn't seen but God
had offered them.

God wants us to look forward to the realization of redemption,
to life in his presence, with great anticipation. He wants us to long
for another world and to anticipate it in faith. And living with
unsatisfaction helps us do that.

Blessings often don't look the way we expect them to. Left to
our wisdom, humans are not quick to seek blessing in curses. But
praise be to God, that's the way things work under his compassion.
We are surprisingly blessed in our hunger and thirst.

EXERCISES

- Read Revelation 21:1–22:5. Let your imagination savor what life
  will be like in our eternal home, free of the curse and fully satisfying.

- Lighten your load in anticipation of the future. Get rid of things
  that tempt you to believe this temporary world is your real home.

- In your own words, rewrite the prayer of Agur son of Jakeh from
  Proverbs 30:8-9. Pray your prayer regularly, asking God to give
  you only what you need so your anticipation will not be dulled
  by a false sense of satisfaction or soured by desperation.

Satisfaction
Is Coming

❧

It was a dusty and frenetic day. It was a day when hope seemed almost visible on the horizon of what once had been a land of promise but was now occupied by brutal outsiders. It was a day whose buoyancy ultimately led to profound disappointment. Oppressed people, driven by desperation for deliverance, stood by the road and cheered as their long-awaited champion rode into the city. Fulfilling ancient prophecy, he rode on a donkey, and they spread their cloaks in the road to make a highway for the king. Though he didn't look much like a deliverer, people dared to believe that this humble man, poor as them, who did not fear either the religious establishment or the political authorities, could be the powerful ruler they had longed for.

And because they had dared to hope on that Sunday, the embarrassment, humiliation, and disenchantment of Friday must have been crushing. Jesus' death seemed to reveal him as a weak man after all. Just another desert wanderer with quick wit and big promises, crushed by the iron fist of Rome. And to think they had almost made him their king.

In this year's Palm Sunday sermon, as in many others, I heard a familiar message: the trouble with that scene on the road was that the people expected the wrong kind of king. They expected a mighty conqueror; Jesus had no interest in building a kingdom on earth. They expected a military hero; Jesus was a lamb ready for sacrifice. They expected swift retribution on their behalf, from a righteous and terrible judge. Jesus was not even willing to defend himself. He was a spiritual hero, not a political one. They needed to adjust their expectations.

But while it's true they had erroneous expectations, I think focusing on that shows an incomplete picture of what happened on Palm Sunday. Jesus was not merely unexpected or misunderstood; he was on a very specific mission. Jesus was not merely a spiritual savior; he was a savior in every sense of the word. He was not disinterested in freeing people from injustice and oppression; he was biding his time. Because his sacrifice had not yet paved the way for forgiveness, the world was not ready for God's justice. History was not yet ripe for revelation of the Son of God in all his glory.

Someday Jesus will reveal himself as the warrior king and righteous judge, and it will mean the end of the world as we know it. The expectations of Palm Sunday will be met in overwhelming fashion—and then some. God does not disappoint people who come to him on his terms, seeking his righteousness, justice, or power. The people of ancient Jerusalem didn't really have the wrong expectations; they were jumping the gun and thinking too small.

Most of the time when I picture Jesus, I think of him the way he looked on the flannelgraph board that served as the backdrop to my childhood in the church. You know the image: white robe, blue sash, sandals, and smiling eyes. I tend to think of him, as I believe most people do, the way he is portrayed in the Gospel passages that describe him healing the sick, multiplying lunches, and patiently teaching people to think in new ways. But this is a tragically incomplete picture of Jesus, overlooking the confrontational rectitude that got him in trouble with the religious elite and ultimately got him killed. It completely misses the picture of Jesus we see elsewhere in the New Testament, after his resurrection: Acts 7, Romans 8, 1 Peter 3, the entire book of Hebrews, and the entire book of Revelation, to name a few. The Jesus we find in these passages is Christ as he is now, seated on a throne in heaven, sovereign over all powers, radiant beyond what our eyes could ever manage to see. And it gets even better. The expectations of those ancient people in Jerusalem who wanted a conquering king will be fulfilled—and the appearance of this king will take our breath away:

> I saw heaven standing open and there before me was a white horse, whose rider is called Faithful and True. With justice he judges and wages war. His eyes are like blazing fire, and on his head are many crowns. He has a name written on him that no one knows but he himself. He is dressed in a robe dipped in blood, and his name is the Word of God. The armies of heaven were following him, riding on white horses and dressed in fine linen, white and clean. Coming out of his mouth is a sharp sword with which to strike down the nations. "He will rule them with an iron scepter." He treads the winepress of the fury of the wrath of God Almighty. On his robe and on his thigh he has this name written:
>
> KING OF KINGS AND LORD OF LORDS. (Revelation 19:11-16)

This is Jesus at his second coming. He will not come as a meek man, hiding his glory in the limitations of humanity. He will not come to bring peace between us; he will come to bring "a sharp sword with which to strike down the nations." He will come to bring an end to human corruption, violence, and foolishness. The one called "Faithful and True" is coming to judge. The "King of kings and Lord of lords" is coming to rule with an iron scepter. Jesus is our conquering military hero after all—not simply over the Roman Empire but over all world empires and all who oppose him. He will fulfill the expectations of those ancient people, but not in the small way they wanted and not before making a way for people to stand in his grace as his justice wipes the world clean.

This same Jesus will fulfill your longings as well. Lest you believe this book is about lowering your expectations of God, let me say clearly that this book is about living unsatisfied not because God will disappoint us but because he will not. Living unsatisfied means living in hope of satisfaction far beyond what we are capable of wanting now. The blessings of unsatisfaction are not only for now. We live in hope deferred. God did not give us these longings for nothing; he gave them with the expectation that we would live in grief, hope, and anticipation.

The sustainable unsatisfied life must be based in hope. And ultimately our only true source of hope is Christ. It's the hope we have for our future that gives us the perspective, ability, and courage to embrace unsatisfaction rather than insist on satisfaction or succumb to despair. Living unsatisfied is not really about self-denial; it's about holding out for true satisfaction. It's not about suppressing our appetites; it's about keeping our appetites sharp in anticipation of a banquet. It's about submitting to delayed gratification, expecting something better. There's really no disappointment or deprivation in it. Seeking satisfaction in this life, on the other hand, is an act of hopelessness. It means giving up on the promise of a greater life beyond this one, the hope of true fulfillment in God's presence.

Demanding satisfaction in this life is asking God to give us what those ancient people asked of Jesus: a temporary solution to a problem we don't understand, a partial response to a crisis that actually requires reinvention of the world. Unsatisfaction helps us remain open to God's fulfilling our hopes and expectations in greater ways than we can possibly wish for.

There's a risk that comes with this unsatisfied life, however. It's not the possibility that we will miss out on something truly good in life by looking forward to something better. This world really doesn't have the answer for us. The real risk is simply that we will get to the end and discover our so-called hope was only foolishness. After all, our hope hinges on the resurrection of Jesus more than two thousand years ago. "And if Christ has not been raised, your faith is futile; you are still in your sins. Then those also who have fallen asleep in Christ are lost. If only for this life we have hope in Christ, we are of all people most to be pitied" (1 Corinthians 15:17-19). This kind of risk is called faith.

If what we have before us is all there is, why not pursue satisfaction at all costs? Without God ruling this world, and without sight of another world to come, our own comfort is as legitimate a pursuit as any. Like they say, you only live once. If something better is not coming, we are the most pathetic people on earth, insisting on living hungry and thirsty.

I haven't been to heaven and back. I haven't found some way to prove the existence of God or unlock the mysteries of the spiritual realm. I can't explain the Trinity to your satisfaction, and I can't tell you where God lives or what he looks like. But I have known God since I was a young child, and I can tell you that I have seen and heard and felt God's presence every year since then. His Word and work have changed me in ways I never could have changed myself. I have learned that he speaks the truth. And I believe. And I am old enough to know that nothing this world has to offer is going to satisfy my soul. I could spend the rest of my days pouring everything in the world into that infinite abyss in my soul, and at the end I would be infinitely miserable. And I could spend my whole life in holy pursuit of my Creator and find myself, at the end, deeply joyful and more unsatisfied with my connection to him.

For all those who, like me, believe and follow Christ, the incompleteness of life in this world is easily tradeable for the one to come. In the meantime, four realities can keep our faith afloat when we are tempted to forget our inheritance and set our sights on shadows.

It's way bigger than us. It takes God's written revelation of himself to help us understand that there is a much larger plan underway in the universe (and beyond it) than we can perceive or understand, although it has a tremendous influence on us. It's easy to believe that we have more control than we do, that our actions have more power than they do, that we will be remembered for the things we want to be remembered for. It's easy to believe that human history is about humans. But God is authoring a story, and while we are the love interest, you and I aren't even major characters. The story is about the author.

Perhaps it's a bit harsh to tell someone, "It's not about you," but we all need to hear and remember that. And there's comfort here too. After all, this means God's plan is impervious to our failings.

This world is temporary. This is cause for grief—especially as we see others around us building their lives on what will wither and fade and be burned to ash. This is also cause for rejoicing because the pain, heartache, sorrow, violence, and hatred in this world will be gone, and it will be made new.

The impermanent nature of this world is simple reality—the most secular empiricist among us will agree that this planet cannot go on forever. The beautiful thing is that while God rested after creating the world, he has not really stopped creating. And at the end of human history he proclaims not destruction but creation: "I am making everything new!" (Revelation 21:5). We are not meant to live as if this is as good as it gets. We are meant to long for the restoration of Eden's pristine beauty, ever-sprouting life, and un-broken fellowship with God.

Some things will last forever. Our friend the writer of Ecclesiastes wrote, "I know that everything God does will endure forever; nothing can be added to it and nothing taken from it" (3:14). Not everything will pass away. Despite our appearance, humans are eternal creatures. Our loving investment in each other will last. Our acts of service are stored as treasure in heaven (Matthew 6:20). Good work done in God's name will be eternally rewarded (Colossians 3:23-24). Our worship will echo through God's heavenly throne room, where our prayers rise like incense (Revelation 5:8). What we spend in knowing, loving, and living for God is an eternal investment that will last and pay rich dividends in a place where no one will live for wealth.

We will be satisfied. Jesus' words in Matthew 5:6 don't simply pronounce empty words of blessing over those who are hungry and thirsty for righteousness. They give a very good reason these folks should consider themselves blessed: "They will be filled."

We can more easily accept the unsatisfied life when we know satisfaction is coming. People in pain find hope in knowing their suffering will be relieved in heaven. Those of us who are painfully aware of the emptiness of temporal comforts can find hope in knowing we will someday be full.

In a sense, living unsatisfied is an exercise in delayed gratifi-cation, a skill that studies have shown to be powerful in helping people live well. In fact, famous research dating back to the 1960s and 1970s established that children who chose delayed gratification went on to become more successful in life. These children were able to exercise self-discipline and resist eating a marshmallow, on the promise that they would be rewarded with a second marshmallow if they waited. Follow-up studies showed that the children who waited enjoyed higher academic achievement, better social skills, lower levels of obesity, and other positive outcomes.

The man behind this research, Walter Mischel, conducted a second study with a different group of children, this time giving them suggestions for passing the time while they tried not to eat the marshmallow. Some were told to think about the delicious attributes of marshmallows; some were supposed to consider the similarities between marshmallows and clouds. A third group was asked to think about the pleasures of pretzels. The most successful in delaying gratification were the children who thought about pretzels. Rather than focus their minds on the pleasure before them, they put their attention elsewhere. "In other words," writes Dr. Alex Lickerman, "one of the most effective ways to distract ourselves from a tempting pleasure we don't want to indulge is by focusing on *another pleasure*." When faced with the temptation to seek full satisfaction in what we can enjoy here and now, one of the most powerful ways we can respond is to focus on the satisfaction to come.

Revelation 22 tells us our eternal home will be a place of unbroken fellowship with God. God's people will live in the light of his presence—literally, with no other source of light necessary. We will engage in completely satisfying work, unified relationships, and a great celebration of all kinds of diversity. It will be a place of so much abundance that no conservation will be necessary; the building materials and pavements will be made of elements we now consider rare and precious. This home will be so secure the city gates will never be closed. Life will flow in the river and grow on the trees. It will be Eden restored, a place of the kind of perfect beauty we ache for.

As Hebrews 13:14 reminds us, this world is not our ultimate home. That doesn't mean our lives on this planet don't matter; they matter more because we will live beyond their limits. The way we live now is infinitely important, even as we look forward to "the city that is to come." So for now, let us live lives marked by meaning, fulfillment, pleasure, contentment—and unsatisfaction.

Let us not deny our hunger for a world made right or reject our thirst for an end to the rebellion in our own hearts. Let us cultivate the habit of desiring God's glory and the fulfillment of his plans rather than our own. Let us habitually believe all those desires will be met in glorious fashion. For those of us who tend such longings, our future will be completely satisfying. We will never go hungry; we will never pant with unsatisfied thirst. We will no longer fill our days with pointless activity; we will not chase after things that will destroy us. The infinite abyss within us will be filled with infinite righteousness and unfailing love, and our restless souls will be truly at home.

In our satisfying future, our appetites will be sated and we will want no more. I think it's possible those who have been really in touch with their hunger and thirst in this life will be more dazzled by the abundance available in the next. Proverbs 27:7 tells us, "One who is full loathes honey from the comb, but to the hungry even what is bitter tastes sweet." Perhaps satisfaction will be sweeter for those who are familiar with their appetites—and for those who have cultivated a taste for the eternal.

Discussion Guide

CHAPTER 1: JESUS DOESN'T WANT YOU TO BE SATISFIED . . . YET

- Where have you heard the message that people who come to Jesus will be completely satisfied here and now?

- What do you think of the author's claim that a relationship with Christ may not bring satisfaction or happiness—at least in complete and lasting form?

- Why is it that growing deeper in faith can make us less—not more—satisfied with life as we know it?

- What do you learn about satisfaction through considering the lives of people in the Bible?

- What does unsatisfaction look like in your life?

CHAPTER 2: SUSTAINABLE FAITH IS UNSATISFIED

- What's your reaction to this quote from the author: "Something is wrong if we feel deeply satisfied, or believe we are satisfied, in this life"?

- How has seeking satisfaction hurt you or people you know?

- What are your thoughts on the idea that our sinful natures are crucified but not yet dead?

- Discuss the differences between dissatisfaction and unsatisfaction. How have you seen these differences in your own life? How might you need to adjust your expectations to reject dissatisfaction and embrace unsatisfaction?

- What experiences in your life have helped make your own faith sustainable, something that can survive hardship and the test of time?

CHAPTER 3: CURSES AND BLESSINGS

- Why is it important to acknowledge that we are unsatisfied because we live under a curse of our own choosing?

- When have you been guilty of focusing so much on the blessings of life with Christ that you forget we still living under a curse for now? What is the harm in ignoring the curse?

- How are you living with false expectations for life or the world around you (life should be easy; I should be happy all the time; God doesn't let his people suffer)? What do you need to do to address these faulty beliefs?

- Discuss the author's basic definition of blessing: "Good things intentionally given." What does this mean to you? Where do you see this in the Bible? How have you experienced it in your own life?

- What is the difference between being blessed and feeling blessed? What does it mean to be hungry and thirsty for righteousness? How is that a blessed life?

CHAPTER 4: HOW TO LIVE
THE UNSATISFIED LIFE

- What does it mean to look into our own internal abyss? What might that look like? What makes it important?

- The author claims people tend to order their lives around avoiding what they fear. When have you done this? What is frightening about living an intentionally unsatisfied life?

- Discuss this quote from the author: "We can and do live without complete satisfaction because we have great hope." What does this hope look like? What do you already know about your capacity for an unsatisfying life?

- How can good things in our lives (family, friends, work, good works) serve as unhealthy and inadequate substitutes for true satisfaction?

- How does embracing unsatisfaction give us the opportunity to be more intentional with our lives and our choices? How can you cultivate unsatisfaction in your life?

CHAPTER 5: ENJOY A MEANINGFUL LIFE

- How can abandoning the pursuit of satisfaction help us find more meaning in our lives?

- Discuss your reaction to the discovery that happiness that lacks deeper meaning (hedonic happiness) is actually harmful to our health. Why is meaning so important to human well-being?

- How do you react to the idea that your life makes an impact on other people, whether or not you're aware of it? How can you take ownership of your impact?

- How can you find meaning in the idea that your life will leave a legacy for those who come after?

- Discuss the analogy of redemption as polishing silver—recognizing the value in what is tarnished and bringing it forth. What needs to be redeemed in your life? How might God bring meaning to your life through this redemption?

CHAPTER 6: LOOK FOR FULFILLMENT

- Have you ever known someone who seems to believe God wants us to be miserable? Have you ever felt this way yourself? What do you think of the idea that self-denial doesn't necessarily mean we don't get what we want?

- What examples come to mind when you think of a person whose life is out of alignment? When have you experienced this kind of conflict, either with your environment or within yourself? What does it mean to bring our lives into alignment with our calling as Christians?

- What do you know about your own unique sense of purpose? How might you come to a better understanding of what you're here for?

- Do the people you interact with on a regular basis reinforce or contradict the values that are most important to you? How might you bring a greater sense of alignment to the relationships in your life?

- How is fulfillment different from true satisfaction? How can you pursue a fulfilling life without expecting it to completely satisfy you?

CHAPTER 7: APPRECIATE THE GIFT OF PLEASURE

- What do you think about the idea that pleasure is a good gift from God that must be kept in its proper place? What does it mean to keep pleasure in its place?

- How have you experienced desire as a good, God-honoring thing in your life?

- Have you experienced "thriver's guilt"? When have you seen it in someone else? How does this kind of guilt hold people back from enjoying and making the most of life?

- Discuss this quote from the author: "So if pleasure is a good thing, and good for us, why are we so nervous about it and so often warned against enjoying it?"

- The author suggests we let pleasure live alongside the harsher realities of life, learning to enjoy ourselves even when we are very aware of suffering and imperfection. What does this look like in practical terms? How can enjoying pleasure increase our appetite for God's better gifts to come?

CHAPTER 8: EMBRACE CONTENTMENT

- The author claims, "For now, contentment is necessary precisely because we are unsatisfied." What does this statement mean to you? Do you agree or disagree? What is the relationship between contentment and living an unsatisfied life?

- When have you experienced contentment? How easily does contentment come for you?

- In Proverbs 30:8, Agur son of Jakeh asks God to "give me neither poverty nor riches, but give me only my daily bread." What is the value in having only what we need and nothing more? How do both poverty and riches undermine our contentment?

- How has other people's complaining affected your life? Your own complaining?

- How does feeding the right appetites lead to contentment? What kinds of appetites do you want to feed in your own life?

CHAPTER 9: SATISFACTION IS COMING

- What does it do for you to consider the picture of Jesus in Revelation 19:11-16? How does this knowledge influence the way you see your own future?

- The author writes, "Lest you believe this book is about lowering your expectations of God, let me say clearly that this book is about living unsatisfied not because God will disappoint us but because he will not." What does this mean? How does our coming satisfaction influence your attitude toward life today?

- If seeking satisfaction in this life is an act of hopelessness, how can you maintain the sense of hope that will help you embrace unsatisfaction?

- The author points to the risk of living with deferred satisfaction and calls it faith. What is risky about faith?

- Proverbs 27:7 says, "One who is full loathes honey from the comb, but to the hungry even what is bitter tastes sweet." How will you keep yourself hungry for full satisfaction?

Notes

CHAPTER 1: JESUS DOESN'T WANT
YOU TO BE SATISFIED . . . YET

7   *God intends for you to be satisfied*: Available online at www.yehweh
.us/2013/12/live-satisfied-life-god-designed-just.html.

God wants you to live: Joel Osteen, *Your Best Life Now: 7 Steps to
Living at Your Full Potential*, 10th Anniversary Ed. (New York:
FaithWords, 2014).

8   *God cares about everything*: Joyce Meyer, "Are You Content with Your
Life?" *Christian Post*, July 21, 2014, www.christianpost.com/news
/are-you-content-with-your-life-123411.

I encourage you: Joyce Meyer, "He's Everything We Need to Be,"
Joyce Meyer Ministries, www.joycemeyer.org/everydayanswers/ea
-teachings/he-is-everything-we-need-to-be. Accessed September
25, 2017.

My life was hijacked: Donna Mikkin, "How Winning the Lottery
Led to Emotional Bankruptcy," C-Suite Network, May 26, 2014,
http://c-suitenetwork.com/blog/2014/05/winning-lottery-led
-emotional-bankruptcy.

9   *I'd have been better off broke*: Melissa Chan, "Here's How Winning
the Lottery Makes You Miserable," *Time*, January 12, 2016, http://
time.com/4176128/powerball-jackpot-lottery-winners.

Experience stretching: Jonah Lehrer, "Why Money Makes You Unhappy," *Wired*, July 21, 2010, www.wired.com/2010/07/happiness
-and-money-2.

The thrill of winning the lottery: Melissa Dahl, "A Classic Psychology
Study on Why Winning the Lottery Won't Make You Happier,"
New York Magazine: The Science of Us, January 13, 2016, http://
nymag.com/scienceofus/2016/01/classic-study-on-happiness-and
-the-lottery.html.

11   *All men seek happiness*: Blaise Pascal, *Pensées*, "Section VII: Morality and Doctrine," available online at www.ccel.org/ccel/pascal/pensees .viii.html.

      But example teaches us little: Ibid.

12   *What is it, then, that this desire*: Ibid.

      There is a God-shaped vacuum: This quotation is erroneously attributed to Pascal in a variety of places, including Thinkexist.com; http://thinkexist.com/quotation/there_is_a_god_shaped_vacuum _in_the_heart_of/166425.html.

13   *Thou hast formed us*: *The Confessions of Saint Augustine*, trans. J. G. Pilkington (Edinburgh: T&T Clark, 1876), book 1, chap. 1.

      Oh! how shall I find rest in thee: Ibid., book 1, chap. 5.

      And sometimes thou dost introduce me: Ibid., book 10, chap. 40.

14   *When once we get intimate*: Oswald Chambers, *My Utmost for His Highest* (Westwood, NJ: Barbour, 1963), January 7 entry.

15   *Contentment is the cultivation*: Jeff Manion, *Satisfied* (Grand Rapids: Zondervan, 2013), 26.

19   *Thirsty persons*: John Gill, *Gill's Exposition of the Entire Bible*, available online at http://biblehub.com/commentaries/gill/john/4 .htm. Accessed March 25, 2017.

      It must not be understood: Marvin R. Vincent, *Vincent's Word Studies*, available online at http://biblehub.com/commentaries/vws/john/4. htm. Accessed March 25, 2017.

21   *Was Jesus satisfied by his life in the world*: See Matthew 15:16; 16:9; 22:18; Mark 8:21; 11:15-17; 14:27; Luke 9:57-62; 19:41-44; 22:31.

CHAPTER 2: SUSTAINABLE FAITH IS UNSATISFIED

32   *It seems to me Paul is saying*: Pastor Ray Kollbocker, "Self-Control," sermon, Parkview Community Church, Glen Ellyn, Illinois, October 18, 2015.

37   *People who are disappointed*: Michael Ashworth, PhD, "Dealing with Disappointment," Psych Central, May 27, 2016, http://psychcentral .com/lib/dealing-with-disappointment.

40   *Belief in God fills an emotional void*: Adam Lee, "There Is No God-Shaped Hole," Daylight Atheism (blog), September 16, 2009, www

.patheos.com/blogs/daylightatheism/2009/09/there-is-no-god
-shaped-hole.

43   *When most oppressed*: George MacDonald, *Unspoken Sermons* (New
      York: Cosimo Classics, 2007), 209-10.

CHAPTER 3: CURSES AND BLESSINGS

53   *This memory of Eden:* Sting, "Desert Rose," *Brand New Day*, A&M,
      1999.

      Happiness dependent on expectations: Keith Wagstaff, "Happiness
      Equation Solved: Lower Your Expectations," *Today*, August 4, 2014,
      www.today.com/health/happiness-equation-solved-lower-your
      -expectations-1D80018852.

58   *God bless his people when*: M. G. Easton, *Illustrated Bible Dictionary*,
      3rd ed. (London: Thomas Nelson & Sons, 1897).

      A state of happiness: William E. Brown, "Blessing," in *Baker's Evan-
      gelical Dictionary of Biblical Theology*, ed. Walter A. Elwell (Grand
      Rapids: Baker, 1996), available online at www.biblestudytools.com/
      dictionaries/bakers-evangelical-dictionary/blessing.html.

      The Greek word markarios: Greek meaning and word-study infor-
      mation accessed through BibleHub.com, http://biblehub.com/
      greek/3107.htm.

59   *These surprising statements of blessing*: Lawrence O. Richards, *Bible
      Reader's Companion* (Colorado Springs: Cook, 2002), 606.

60   *A state not of inner feeling*: W. C. Allen, *The International Critical Com-
      mentary: A Critical and Exegetical Commentary on the Gospel According
      to St. Matthew* (New York: Charles Scribner's Sons, 1907), 39.

61   *They shall be satisfied*: Albert Barnes, *Notes on the Bible* (1834),
      available online at www.sacred-texts.com/bib/cmt/barnes/mat005
      .htm. Accessed March 25, 2017.

CHAPTER 4: HOW TO LIVE THE UNSATISFIED LIFE

65   *Even if I wanted to go: Dr. Seuss' How the Grinch Stole Christmas*,
      directed by Ron Howard (Universal City, CA: Universal Pictures,
      2000).

75   *Our food preferences are*: Kirsten Keane, "In Good Taste: Research
      Explores Food Preferences," *Research Matters*, April 5, 2010,

https://research.asu.edu/stories/read/good-taste-research-explores-food-preferences.

75   *Changing preferences as adults*: Oliver Thring, "Changing Tastes: The Wandering Palate," *The Guardian*, US Edition, June 22, 2012, www.theguardian.com/lifeandstyle/wordofmouth/2012/jun/22/changing-tastes-the-wandering-palate.

76   *Gratitude changes brain chemistry*: Alex Korb, "The Grateful Brain," *Psychology Today*, November 20, 2012, www.psychologytoday.com/blog/prefrontal-nudity/201211/the-grateful-brain.

      Gratitude builds resilience: Amy Morin, "7 Scientifically Proven Benefits of Gratitude," *Psychology Today*, April 3, 2015, www.psychologytoday.com/blog/what-mentally-strong-people-dont-do/201504/7-scientifically-proven-benefits-gratitude.

77   *when the sun's shining*: Matt Redman, "Blessed Be Your Name," *Where Angels Fear to Tread*, Survivor, 2002.

84   *All that glitters is not gold*: William Shakespeare, *The Merchant of Venice*, act II, scene VII.

      Money never made a man happy: Available online at www.bartleby.com/349/authors/77.html.

85   *Can't buy me love*: The Beatles, "Can't Buy Me Love," *A Hard Day's Night*, Capitol, 1964.

      Chasing after this world: Newsboys, "Live with Abandon," *Restart*, Sparrow Records, 2013.

      I still haven't found: U2, "I Still Haven't Found What I'm Looking For," *The Joshua Tree*, Island Records, 1987.

86   *Turn your eyes upon Jesus*: Helen Howarth Lemmel, "Turn Your Eyes Upon Jesus," 1922.

CHAPTER 5: ENJOY A MEANINGFUL LIFE

88   *Empty positive emotions*: Emily Esfahani Smith, "Meaning Is Healthier Than Happiness," *Atlantic*, August 1, 2013, www.theatlantic.com/health/archive/2013/08/meaning-is-healthier-than-happiness/278250.

93   *Interpreting the original language of Exodus 34:6-7*: See www.biblestudytools.com/lexicons/hebrew/kjv/paqad.html.

93 *Breakthrough scientific study*: Alice G. Walton, "How Health and Lifestyle Choices Can Change Your Genetic Make-Up," *Atlantic*, November 6, 2011, www.theatlantic.com/health/archive/2011/11/how-health-and-lifestyle-choices-can-change-your-genetic-make-up/247808.

    Lifestyle choices can change DNA: "Weekend Alcohol Consumption May Cause Damage to DNA," Fox News, January 2, 2014, www.foxnews.com/health/2014/01/02/weekend-alcohol-consumption-may-cause-damage-to-dna; Dan Hurley, "Grandma's Experiences Leave a Mark on Your Genes," *Discover Magazine*, May 2013, http://discovermagazine.com/2013/may/13-grandmas-experiences-leave-epigenetic-mark-on-your.genes.

101 *When once we get intimate*: Oswald Chambers, *My Utmost for His Highest* (Westwood, NJ: Barbour, 1963), January 7 entry.

103 *We are created to enjoy relationships*: See Ecclesiastes 4:7-12; Romans 12:4-5; 1 Corinthians 12:12-26; Galatians 6:1-3; Colossians 3:12-15; 1 John 4:7-12.

103 *I cannot begin to understand*: Gillian Marchenko, *Still Life: A Memoir of Living Fully with Depression* (Downers Grove, IL: InterVarsity Press, 2016), 132.

CHAPTER 6: LOOK FOR FULFILLMENT

106 *Although easily corrupted*: Jen Pollock Michel, *Teach Us to Want* (Downers Grove, IL: InterVarsity Press, 2014), 200-201.

109 *Recognizing that we are acting in opposition*: Dana Gionta, "Integrity and Employee Well-Being," *Psychology Today*, April 6, 2010, www.psychologytoday.com/blog/occupational-hazards/201004/integrity-and-employee-well-being.

110 *The symptoms of psychological stress*: Edward A. Dreyfus, "Integrity, Relationships, and Your Mental Health: Part 2 of 3," http://docdreyfus.com/psychologically-speaking/integrity-relationships-and-your-mental-health-part-2-of-3.

CHAPTER 7: APPRECIATE THE GIFT OF PLEASURE

125 *Never forget that when we are dealing*: C. S. Lewis, *A Year with C. S. Lewis: Daily Readings from His Classic Works* (New York: HarperCollins, 2003), 331.

132   *Optimal income for happiness*: Jennifer Robison, "Happiness Is Love—and $75,000," *Gallup Business Journal,* November 17, 2011, www.gallup.com/businessjournal/150671/happiness-is-love-and -75k.aspx.

133   *happiness is the truth*: Pharrell Williams, "Happy," *Girl*, Columbia Records, 2014.

135   *An unsatisfied desire*: C. S. Lewis, *Surprised by Joy: The Shape of My Early Life* (Orlando: Houghton Mifflin Harcourt, 1955), 18.

140   *We are far too easily pleased*: C. S. Lewis, *Readings for Meditation and Reflection*, ed. Walter Hooper (New York: HarperSanFrancisco, 1992), 35.

CHAPTER 8: EMBRACE CONTENTMENT

145   *Contentment lies within a man*: Thomas Watson, "Use I. Showing how a Christian may make his life comfortable," in *The Art of Divine Contentment* (Lexington, KY: First Rate Publishers, 2015).

146   *Freedom from wanting more than is good for us*: Richard A. Swenson, *Contentment: The Secret to a Lasting Calm* (Colorado Springs: Nav-Press, 2013), 14.

147   *INFJs are all but defined by their pursuit of ideals*: "INFJ Strengths and Weaknesses," 16 Personalities, www.16personalities.com/infj-strengths -and-weaknesses.

149   *We fail to recognize*: Stephen Grcevich, "The False Gospel and Mental Illness," Key Ministry blog, October 30, 2016, www.keyministry.org /church4everychild/2016/10/30/the-false-gospel-and-mental-illness.

150   *Would we have comfort in our lives*: Watson, "Showing how a Christian," 13.

153   *If you're pinned in a corner*: Minda Zetlin, "Listening to Complainers Is Bad for Your Brain," *Inc.*, August 20, 2012, www.inc.com/minda-zetlin /listening-to-complainers-is-bad-for-your-brain.html.

       The more we complain: Travis Bradberry, "How Complaining Rewires Your Brain for Negativity," *Entrepreneur*, September 9, 2016, www .entrepreneur.com/article/281734.

154   *You keep using that word*: *The Princess Bride*, directed by Rob Reiner (Century City, CA: 20th Century Fox, 1987).

CHAPTER 9: SATISFACTION IS COMING

167   *Exercise in delayed gratification*: James Clear, "40 Years of Stanford Research Found That People with This One Quality Are More Likely to Succeed," personal blog, http://jamesclear.com/delayed -gratification. Accessed April 24, 2017.

168   *One of the most effective ways to distract ourselves*: Alex Lickerman, "The Power of Delaying Gratification," *Psychology Today*, July 29, 2012, www.psychologytoday.com/blog/happiness-in-world/201207/ the-power-delaying-gratification.

About the Author

Amy Simpson is deeply committed to seeing purposeful people make the most of their gifts and opportunities. As an author, speaker, and life and leadership coach, she helps influencers get clear on their calling and thrive in times of transition so they can see clearly, lead boldly, live true, and fully engage in life with guiding purpose.

A creative professional and a former publishing executive, Amy has a heart for leaders who are ready to thrive through change and come out stronger. As a member of a family affected by serious mental illness, she holds strong convictions that each person's life has purpose and that points of crisis are opportunities for transformation. As an experienced leader, filling roles from executive to entrepreneur, she knows how to help others turn challenges into resources.

Whether speaking into a microphone or through the written word, Amy is a gifted communicator with a prophetic voice. She is author of the award-winning books *Troubled Minds: Mental Illness and the Church's Mission* and *Anxious: Choosing Faith in a World of Worry* (both InterVarsity Press). She serves as an editor at large for Christianity Today's CTPastors .com and a regular contributor for various publications.

As a life and leadership coach, Amy is a firm believer that life is too short to waste time living out of sync with God's purposes, and she challenges clients throughout the United States to step into their calling with authenticity and excellence. She specializes in working with people who find themselves on the edge of something new, whether a new role, organization, approach, project, or career.

Amy holds an English degree from Trinity International University, an MBA from the University of Colorado, and CPCC certification from Coaches Training Institute. She loves to travel with her husband, Trevor, their two teenage girls, and their lovable dogs, Rosie Cotton and Samwise. She lives with these wonderful folks in the suburbs of Chicago, where she is committed to perfecting her dry sense of humor and reading nearly everything she can.

You can find Amy at:
Email: contact@amysimpsononline.com
Website: www.amysimpson.com
Facebook: www.facebook.com/amy.simpson.author
Twitter: @aresimpson